TURNER

CECILIA POWELL

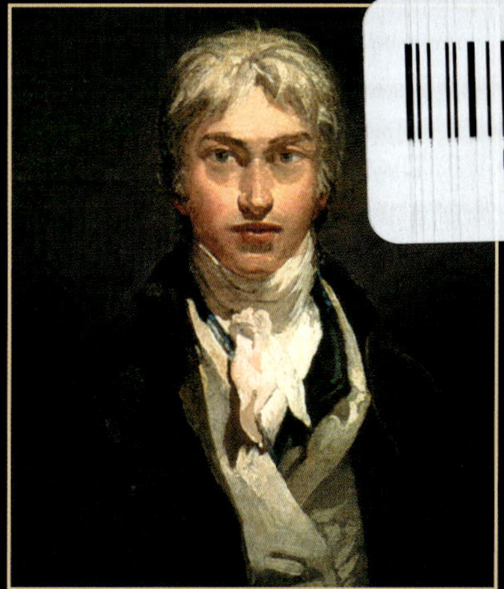

— ABOVE —
*A thoughtful young man,
intent upon success: Turner's
self-portrait of about 1800.*

CONTENTS

— ABOVE —
*Inspired by Italian light
in 1819: San Giorgio Maggiore,
Venice: Morning.*

— FRONT COVER —
*Sail gives way to steam in this
poignant detail from one of
Turner's most famous paintings,*
The Fighting Temeraire
(see page 25).

EARLY LESSONS AND INFLUENCES

Turner was born in 1775 in Maiden Lane, close to London's Covent Garden. He received little schooling but soon displayed a talent for drawing. His father, a barber from Devon, proudly pinned up his work in the shop so that it was noticed by rich and well-connected customers. 'William', he said, 'is going to be a painter!'

In 1789 the boy began attending the free classes of the Royal Academy, then housed nearby, at Somerset House in the Strand. Here he was taught to draw the human figure from plaster casts of statues, and then from living models. He heard lectures from the best British artists of the day, including the first President, Sir Joshua Reynolds (1723–92). In 1790, aged just 15, he had a watercolour accepted for the prestigious annual exhibition.

There were no painting classes at the Academy so Turner continued his own observations and experiments. His studies went hand-in-hand with paid employment and he learned from all he did. He painted scenery for a

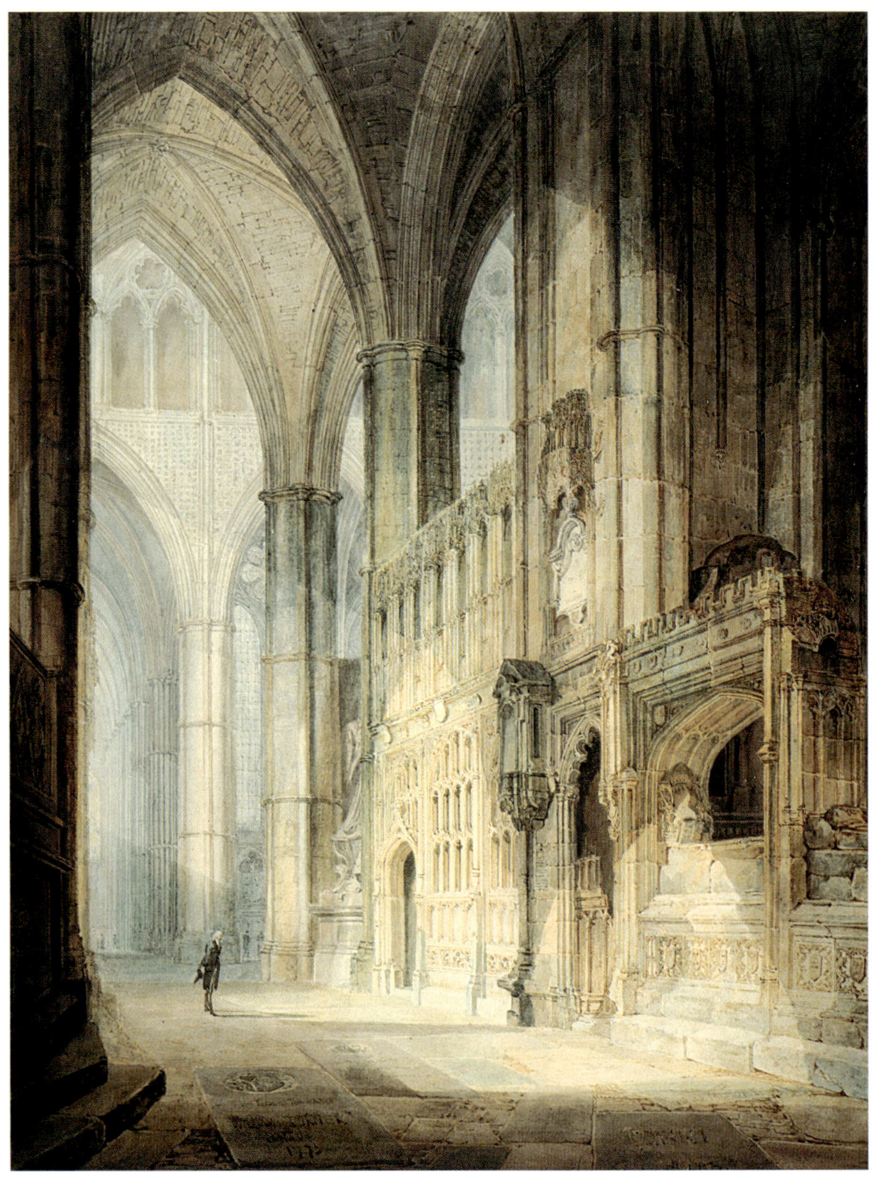

St Erasmus in Bishop Islip's Chapel, Westminster Abbey, 1796. Turner's extra-ordinary skill with water-colours and his ability to paint architectural subjects were quickly recognized. Here he included his own date of birth on a stone in the fore-ground, ensuring that viewers knew he was still only 21.

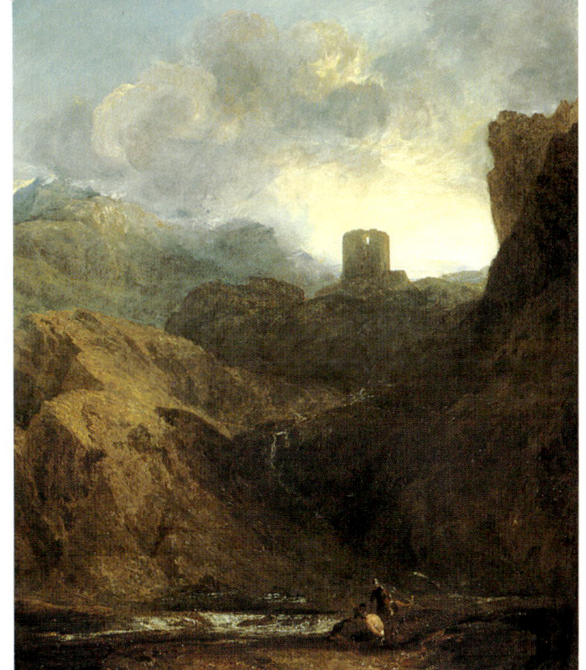

In the 1790s he started painting in oils (more highly regarded than watercolours) and making sketching tours. He began by visiting counties close to London and staying with relations in the West Country but soon went further afield. The outbreak of war between Britain and France in 1793 prevented him going abroad, but he was enthralled by the mountains of Britain itself: the Lake District in 1797, North Wales in 1798 and 1799, Scotland in 1801.

He also fell under the spell of Claude Lorrain, a 17th-century painter much admired and collected in Britain. Claude's depictions of beautiful, ideal landscapes, inspired by Italy and characterized by calm, spaciousness and clarity of light, were a lasting influence and a lifelong challenge.

theatre. He coloured in drawings for Thomas Hardwick, an architect, and helped Thomas Malton, an artist specializing in London views. On winter evenings he copied landscape sketches at an informal academy organized by a well-known collector, Dr Thomas Monro, who provided a small fee and a supper of oysters. His companions there included the equally gifted Thomas Girtin (1775–1802).

Turner's early efforts were soon rewarded. An oil painting of fishing boats by moonlight, *Fishermen at Sea*, was accepted by the Academy in 1796. He was elected an Associate in 1799, at the youngest age allowed, and a full member in 1802. He attracted important patrons. However, life at home was difficult. His only sister had died in 1783 and his mother was unstable: in 1800 she was placed in Bethlem Hospital where she died in 1804.

— ABOVE —

Dolbadern Castle, *painted in 1799–1800, shows the tower in which the Welsh prince Owen Goch was imprisoned in the 13th century. Such subjects, with their emphasis on majestic solitude and the struggle for liberty, were much in vogue at this time.*

— RIGHT —

Turner's early work often shows the influence of Dutch marine painting and he later declared it had 'made me a painter'. Ships bearing up for Anchorage *of 1802 was the first Turner bought by his patron Lord Egremont and it still hangs at Petworth today.*

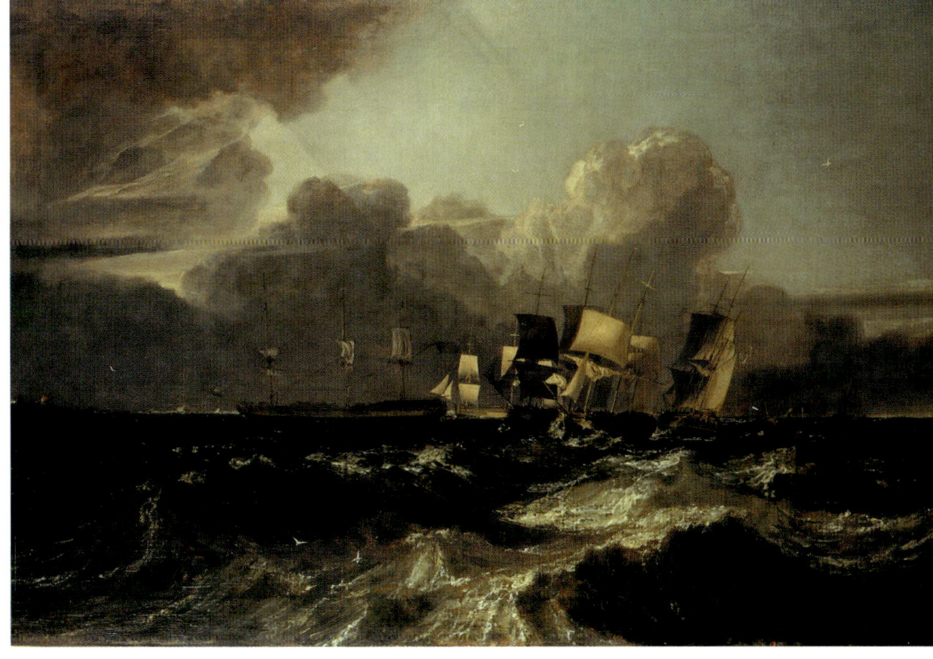

After a peace treaty with France was signed in 1802, many Britons seized the chance to cross the Channel and travel on the Continent. Turner made his way to Paris in July and then on to the Alps before returning to Paris in September. For this first foreign tour he had the support of a travelling companion and the sponsorship of three patrons. He was free to concentrate on his art and he made the most of it.

In Paris he feasted his eyes on paintings – not just those in artists' studios and French collections but the famous masterpieces by Dutch and Italian artists that had been seized from museums, galleries and churches of conquered territories by France's new ruler, Napoleon. The experience was invaluable. Britain had no National Gallery of its own (and did not have one till 1824) and, unlike Catholic churches in continental Europe, British Protestant churches were not filled with images.

Turner's first tour of Switzerland was long and comprehensive, from Geneva in the west to the Great St Bernard Pass, St Gotthard, Lake Lucerne, Zurich and Basle. It afforded his first sight of Mont Blanc and countless other awe-inspiring peaks, glaciers and snowy ranges. He saw violent thunderstorms and the devastation caused by avalanches. He also enjoyed the tranquil beauty of lakes and fertile valleys and a first brief sight of Italy in the environs of Aosta.

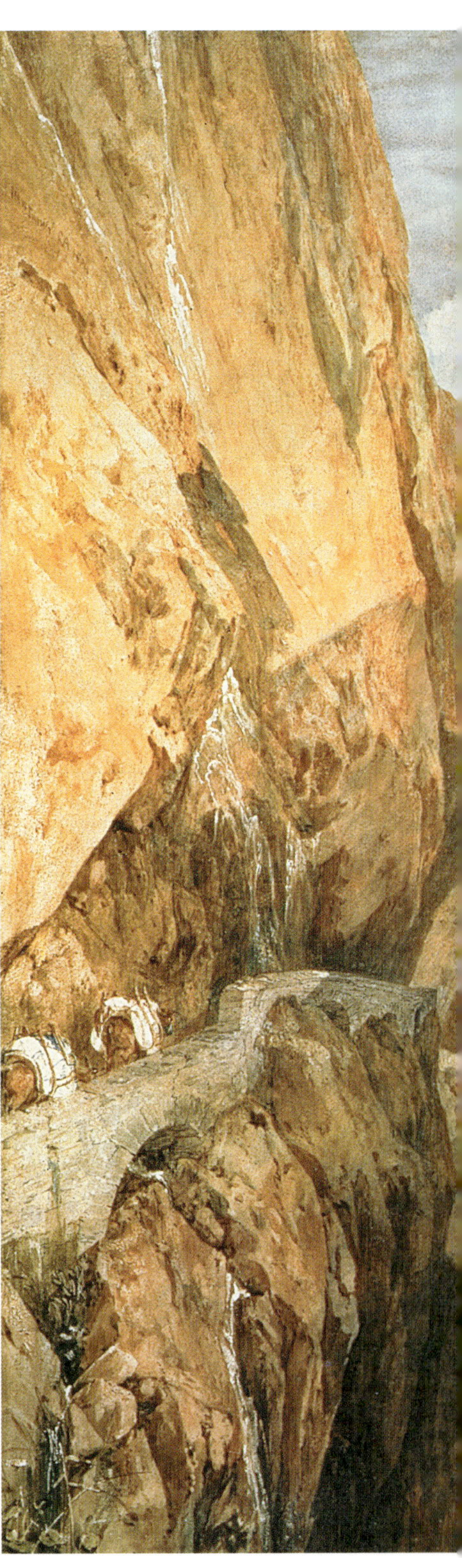

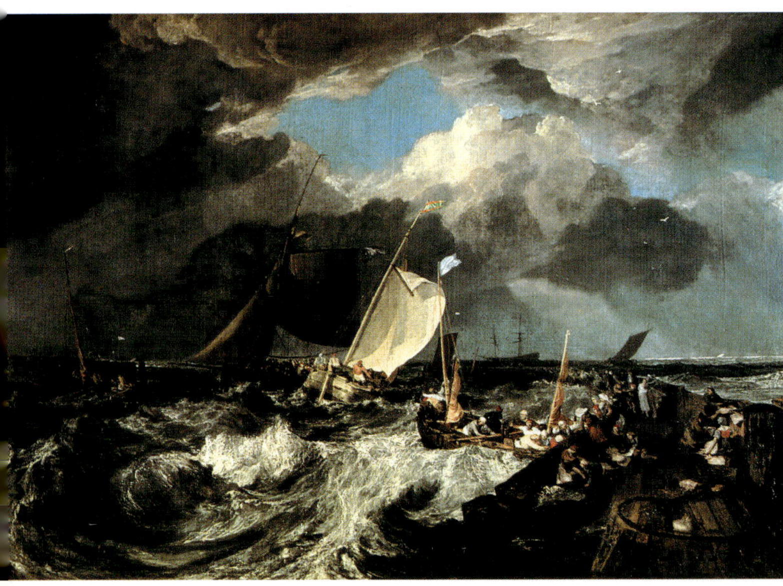

Calais Pier, with French Poissards preparing for Sea: an English Packet arriving. *Turner's sense of pride after his first Channel crossing is clear from this painting in the National Gallery. It illustrates the discomfort and dangers of travel as well as hinting at Anglo-French conflict.*

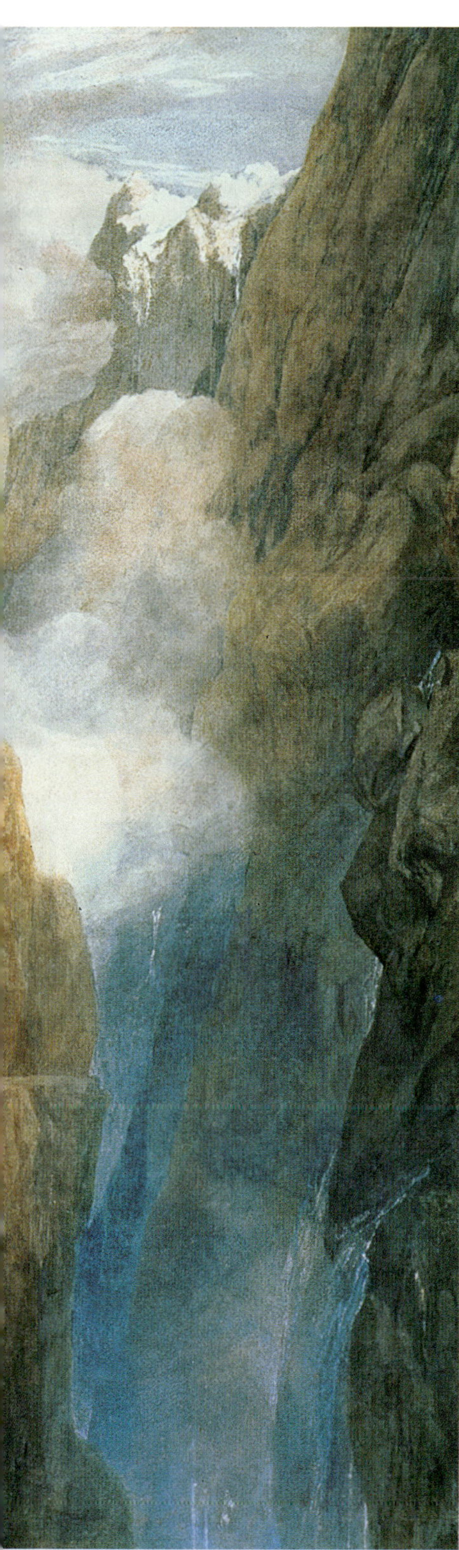

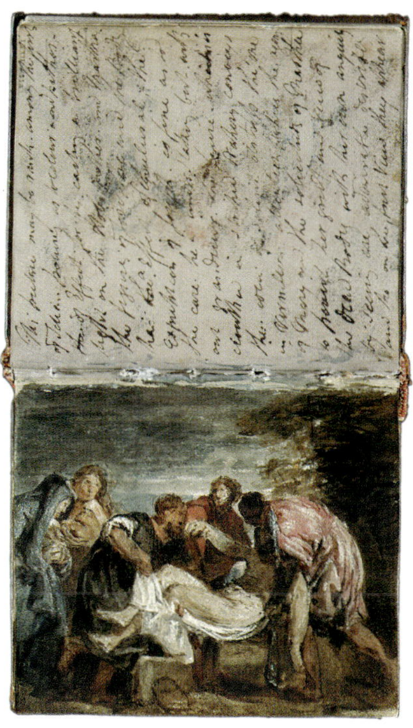

The sensational scenery of the Alps had only recently become a fashionable subject for painters and Turner soon realized the inadequacy of most of their depictions, though he learned much from studying the work of Richard Wilson (1713/14–82) and J.R. Cozens (1752–97). The Alps were to be a favourite theme for the rest of his career. He evolved fresh compositions and experimented with new techniques to evoke the grandeur of their everlasting forms and to capture the constantly changing effects of light. He became the supreme master of rendering them in calm and stormy weather, as benign as well as threatening presences.

He was to cross the Channel many times in his life and his experiences of the sea and deep understanding of seamanship are often reflected in his art. Here, as with his landscapes, his work may refer to the art of the past but is firmly based in the reality of the present. He depicted many shipwrecks and disasters at sea, with vessels tossed by violent winds and waves. By contrast, he often produced marine subjects that magically evoke the tranquillity of sea and shore.

On returning home he used some of his many sketches as the basis for watercolours or oils. Some were produced immediately, to repay his sponsors' generosity, others at leisure for years to come. The war was resumed in 1803 and Turner did not go abroad again till 1817.

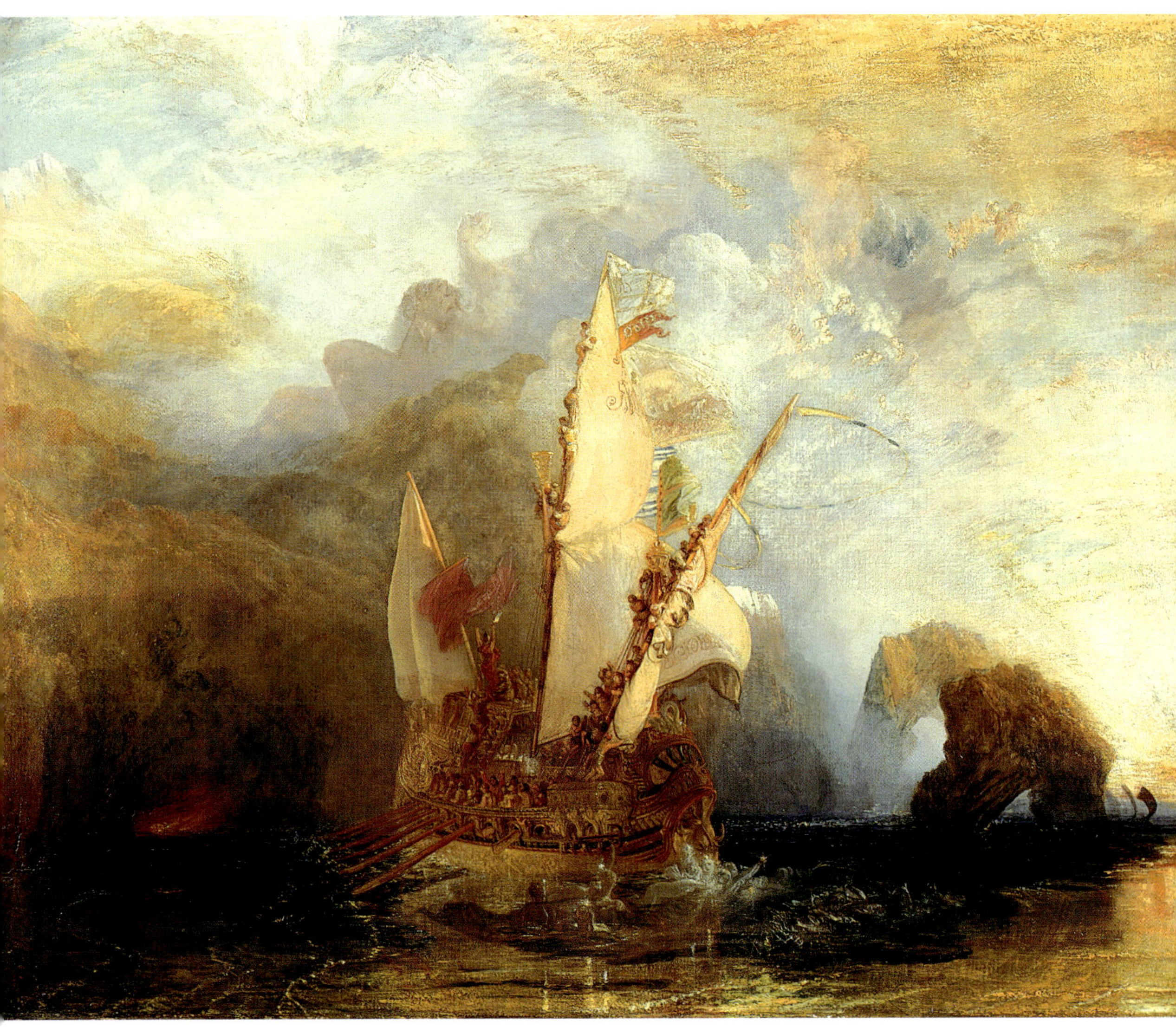

British culture in Turner's day was dominated by the past. Education required, above all, study of the classical world of Greece and Rome, the civilizations that had shaped so many features of western Europe.

At the Royal Academy, founded in 1768, just seven years before Turner himself was born, the most highly regarded category of painting was 'history painting'. This was a broad term comprising scenes from ancient and modern history, the Bible and great literature of all periods. Such themes, with their power to stimulate thought and emotion and foster moral values, were regarded as intellec-tually superior to the mere recording involved in producing landscapes, portraits or still life.

Like countless other artists, Turner painted subjects from the Bible, being especially inspired by graphic accounts of storm and deluge in the Old Testament. Even more important sources were the history and literature of Greece and Rome, especially the epic poems of Homer and Virgil. With their potent mixture of fact and legend (the Trojan War and the events leading to the founding of Rome), together with age-old myths attached to locations around the Mediterranean, Homer's *Odyssey* and Virgil's

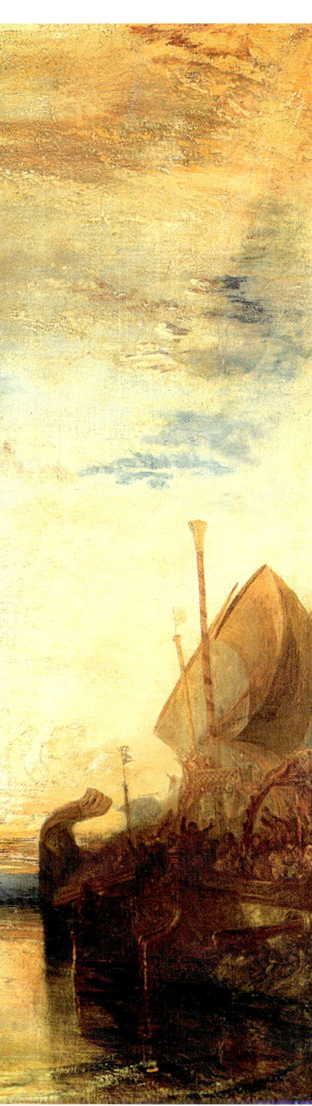

Aeneid were rich sources for a painter with an imagination as vivid as Turner's. They fascinated him for 50 years.

In his 'history paintings', unlike those of other painters, the forces of nature are usually the dominant feature of the scene: a storm-tossed landscape, a serene or turbulent sea, an optimistic dawn or angry sunset. These serve as powerful visible expressions of the emotions at the centre of his story, while the characters mentioned in his title sometimes occupy a relatively small space in the picture itself.

Turner thus shows again and again the drama and frustrations of mankind's ceaseless struggle against the natural world and the elements and – by implication – the blind forces of chance and destiny. For Turner, landscape painting was a crucial element in a picture and a vehicle for expression rather than a mere backdrop.

Turner read widely: classical authors (in translation), Shakespeare, Milton and other English poets, his own contemporaries. He often mentioned his sources in his titles or included quotations in exhibition catalogues. Sometimes he composed his own verses to accompany his works and described these as extracts from a philosophical poem, *Fallacies of Hope*.

— BELOW —
Snow Storm: Hannibal and his Army crossing the Alps. *Although this painting was overtly about the Carthaginian invasion of Italy in the 3rd century* BC, *viewers in 1812 would instantly have seen its relevance to Napoleon's invasion of Italy in recent times and the continuing turmoil of war in Europe.*

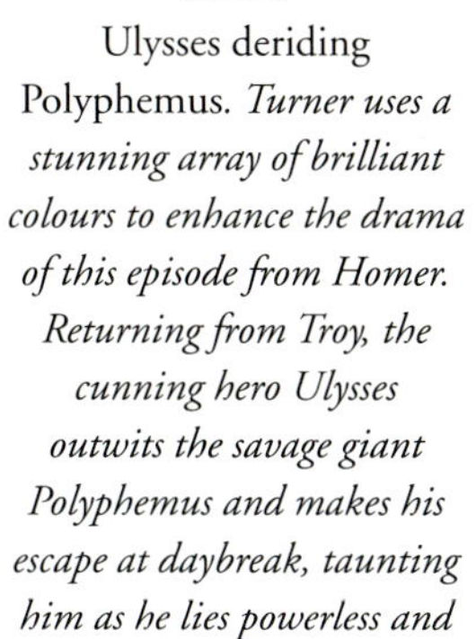

— ABOVE —
Ulysses deriding Polyphemus. *Turner uses a stunning array of brilliant colours to enhance the drama of this episode from Homer. Returning from Troy, the cunning hero Ulysses outwits the savage giant Polyphemus and makes his escape at daybreak, taunting him as he lies powerless and blinded on his cliff.*

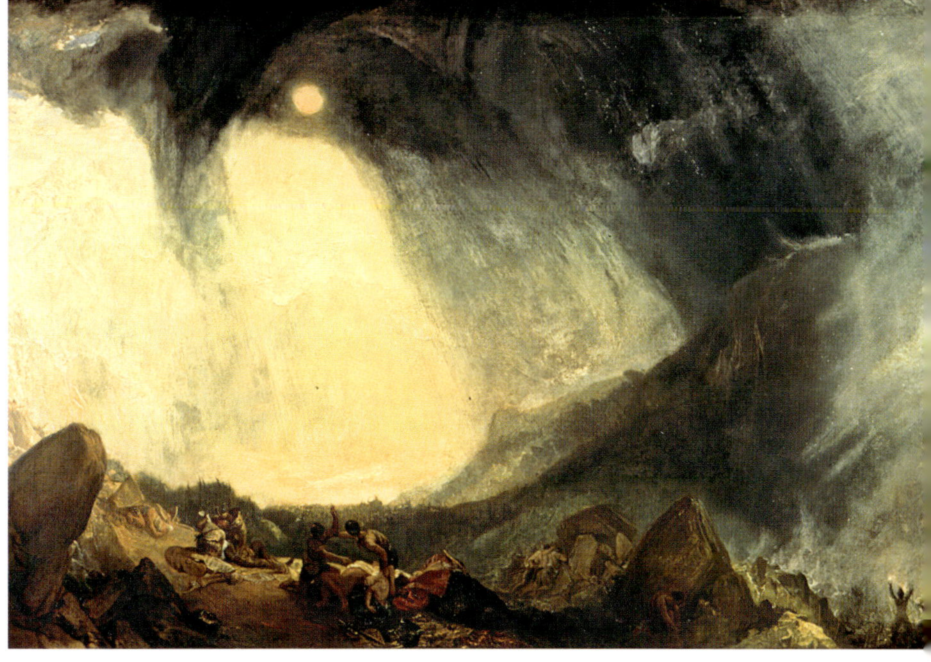

NAPOLEON AND AFTER

The French Revolution in 1789 with its ideals of liberty, equality and fraternity induced a mood of optimism in many other countries. In the lines of the poet William Wordsworth, born in 1770, 'Bliss was it in that dawn to be alive, But to be young was very heaven!' The initial euphoria soon wore off, however, when the revolutionary fervour in France degenerated into the bloody horrors of the Terror and the infant French Republic attacked other nations.

With the rise to power of the military genius Napoleon, French armies embarked on the conquest of Europe and the imposition of modern ideas and institutions. Little of the Continent escaped war. Apart from a short interval in 1802–3, Britain and France remained at war throughout the years of Turner's young manhood – from the winter before his 18th birthday to the summer of 1815 when he was 40 years old.

The British war effort was for many years more successful at sea than on land. Notable naval victories were won, especially by Admiral Nelson, culminating in a decisive victory at Trafalgar in 1805 when Nelson himself was killed.

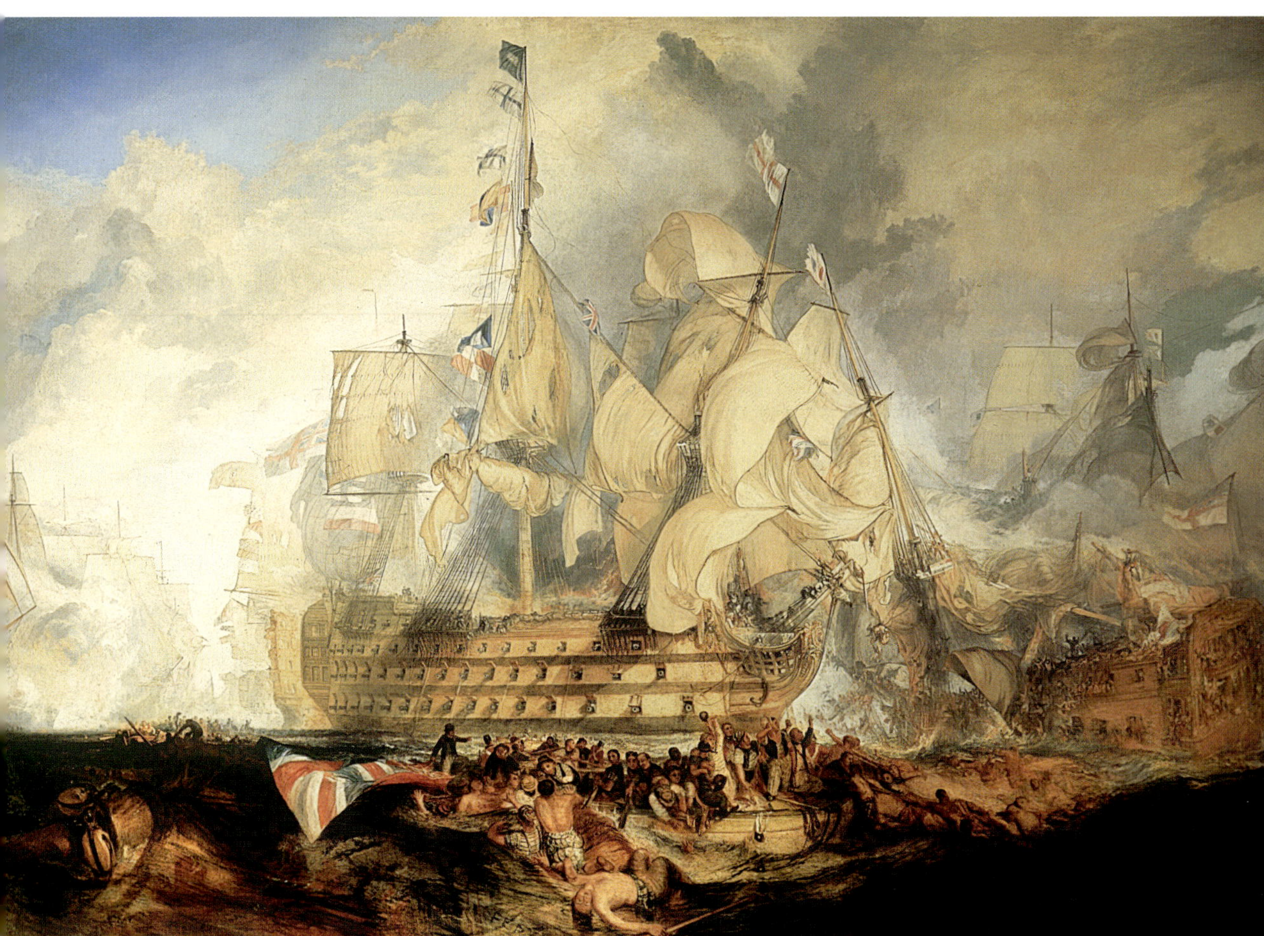

The Battle of Trafalgar. *In 1822 Turner was commissioned by George IV to depict Nelson's victory at Trafalgar. However, his painting was too realistic for the king, and was soon removed from St James's Palace to Greenwich. It is now in the National Maritime Museum.*

Victories in Spain and Portugal won by the Duke of Wellington, combined with Napoleon's disastrous Moscow campaign of 1812, helped bring about the French emperor's downfall. He abdicated in 1814 and was exiled to Elba. His final bid to regain power was defeated by the forces of Britain and Prussia in the greatest battle Europe had experienced, at Waterloo near Brussels, in June 1815. Napoleon was imprisoned for life on the remote Atlantic island of St Helena where he died in 1821.

Waterloo brought in a long period of peace which lasted the rest of Turner's life, allowing him to make regular visits to mainland Europe. There he saw the effects of the wars wherever he went: not just shattered forts and buildings but also the fine new roads and mountain routes constructed by French soldiers.

Turner visited the field of Waterloo two years after the battle. Rather than painting a triumphalist scene, he produced a sombre and compassionate picture of the night after the battle, the ground strewn with the dead and wounded. He exhibited this in 1818 with a moving quotation from *Childe Harold's Pilgrimage* by Lord Byron, the most celebrated poet of the age.

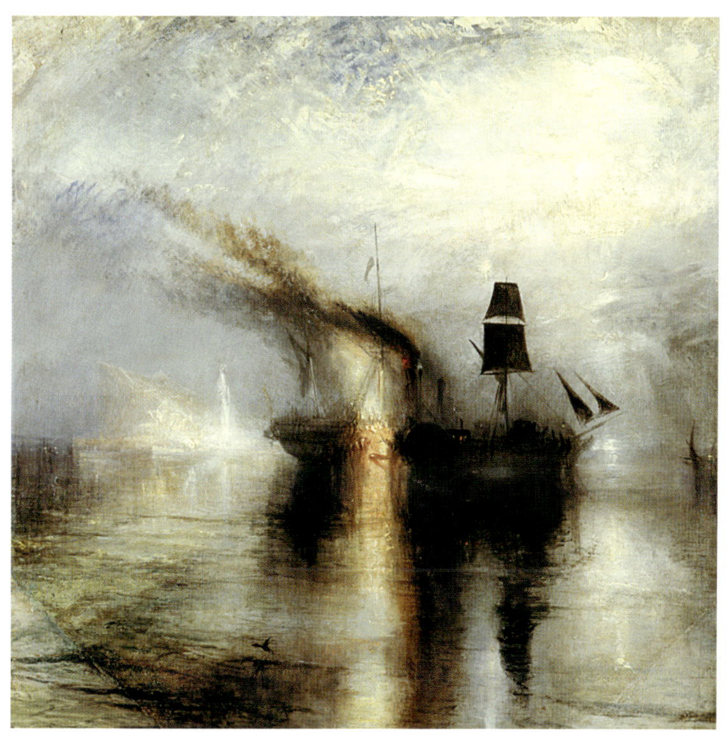

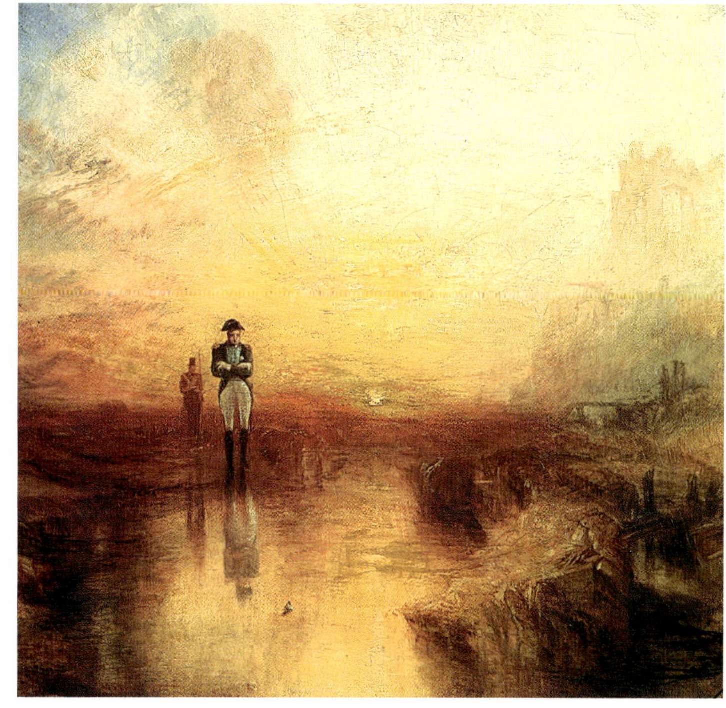

METHODS AND MATERIALS

All Turner's materials came from natural sources. He painted on canvas, wooden panels and paper, experimenting with many different kinds. His papers were manufactured from old rags – discarded items of linen, hemp or cotton which were processed in paper mills.

His colouring materials, or pigments, were derived from animal, vegetable or mineral sources. They were available ready-made from 'colourmen' in solid form and ground into powder. Paint was freshly created each time by mixing the pigments on a palette: with water for watercolours or linseed oil for paintings. When travelling, he could take compressed cakes of colour in a pocketbook or prepared pigment-paste in bladders. All these materials were found in his studio after his death.

Turner drew mostly in graphite (or lead black) pencil, sometimes in ink or chalk. He used a variety of hair brushes for different paints and purposes, sometimes helped by his own fingers or thumbnail.

His earliest watercolours were very conventional: he filled in outlines with a small range of muted colours, and painted water, trees and sky according to current formulae.

He soon abandoned all this and became a master of ingenuity and invention. He immersed himself in the study of nature, making sketches out of doors. Back home he developed his ideas on larger sheets of better-quality paper, often working on several scenes at once. In his early twenties he said he drove the colours around till he had expressed the idea in his mind.

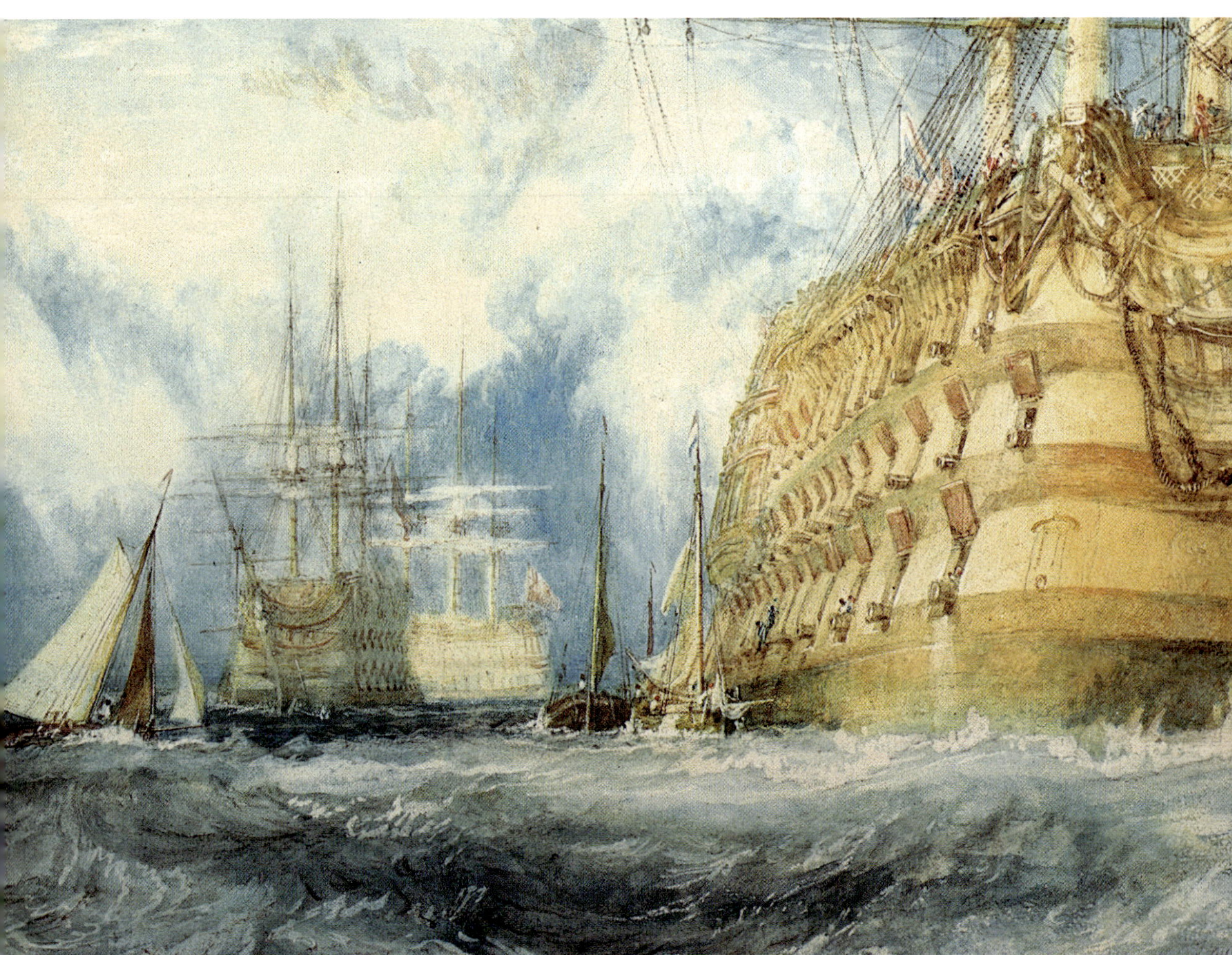

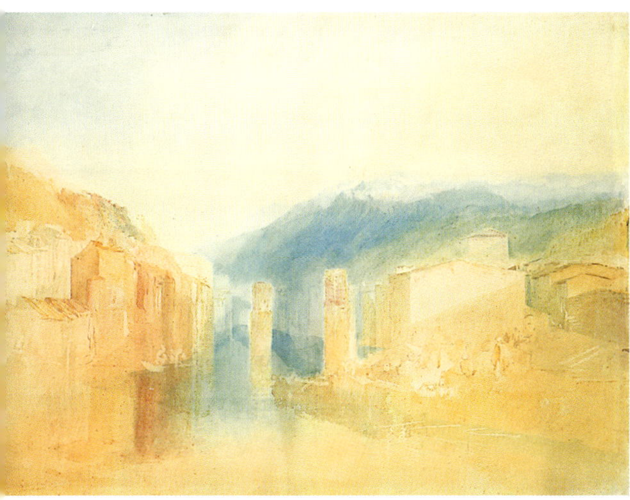

Grenoble Bridge: preparatory study. *Turner planned his watercolours carefully by making studies like this. He would work out a composition based on his pencil sketches, and then test it by blocking in large areas of colour very simply.*

New pigments were introduced throughout Turner's life. He seized on these eagerly when they appeared, eventually using at least a dozen yellows and several reds.

The watercolours of his maturity were begun with layers of thin coloured washes which he overlaid with innumerable minute touches and highlights of bright colour. He achieved a diversity of effects by scratching away paint, sponging it out with blotting paper or bread, using it thinly on a wet surface or dragging a nearly dry brush across the paper. Sometimes he used coloured paper. He mixed lead white with watercolour to produce gouache and could thus create opaque areas of dense colour as well as vaporous transparency.

Turner's range of techniques in oil was equally breathtaking, with infinitely subtle and delicate passages in some works and bold brushwork, the use of the palette knife and thicker paint in others. He used colour itself and colour contrasts to create his paintings, wanting viewers 'to see through the picture into space'.

— LEFT —
A First Rate taking in Stores. *This watercolour was painted in a single morning under the watchful eye of a teenager. Walter Fawkes's son later described how Turner tore, scratched and scrabbled at the paper until he was satisfied. The work is now in the Cecil Higgins Art Gallery, Bedford.*

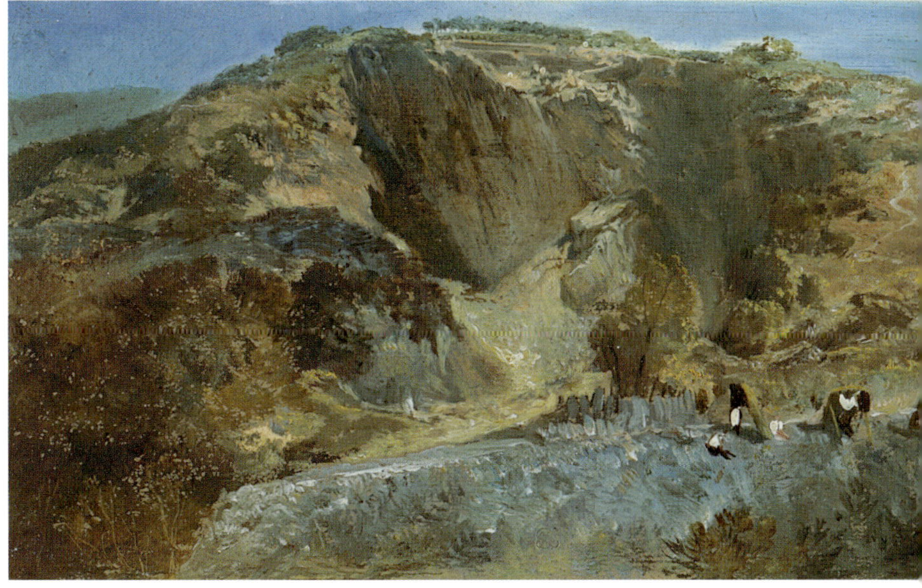

— ABOVE —
A Quarry. *Turner did not usually work in oils in the open air. However, when a friend produced a paintbox and specially prepared paper on a visit to Devon, he could not resist and painted some wonderfully vivid little oil sketches.*

ITALY – COLOUR AND LIGHT

The art and architecture of Italy have attracted foreign-ters for centuries. In Turner's day a study-tour was regarded as vital for painters, architects and sculptors, but because of the war with France he could not manage this until he was 44 years old.

In 1819 he finally set off for Rome and was away for six months. It was the longest tour of his life. Like earlier well-born Grand Tourists, he followed a circular route to see as much as possible, visiting Venice, Florence and other historic cities and beauty spots. He stayed about two months in Rome, with excursions into its countryside and south to Naples and Pompeii. His days were spent looking and learning and he filled 22 sketchbooks with notes and drawings. Besides recording all manner of sights in town and country, from ancient ruins to modern costumes, he observed light and colour very closely. He also paid attention to the great works of art in Italian galleries.

Most of his sketches were made in pencil for the sake of speed – he said a coloured sketch took as long as 15 in pencil. Colours were noted in writing, stored in his memory and experimented with indoors where the light was less volatile and he was away from prying eyes.

After his experience of Italy and the Mediterranean, Turner's interest in light became stronger than ever and he became notorious for his use of yellow. Critics made disparaging remarks suggesting he used mustard, eggs or cream rather than oil paint.

The brilliant light of the Mediterranean inspired some radiant sketches in 1819, including The Bay of Naples and Vesuvius. *Turner drew in pencil out of doors, then worked his sketches up in watercolour back at his lodgings.*

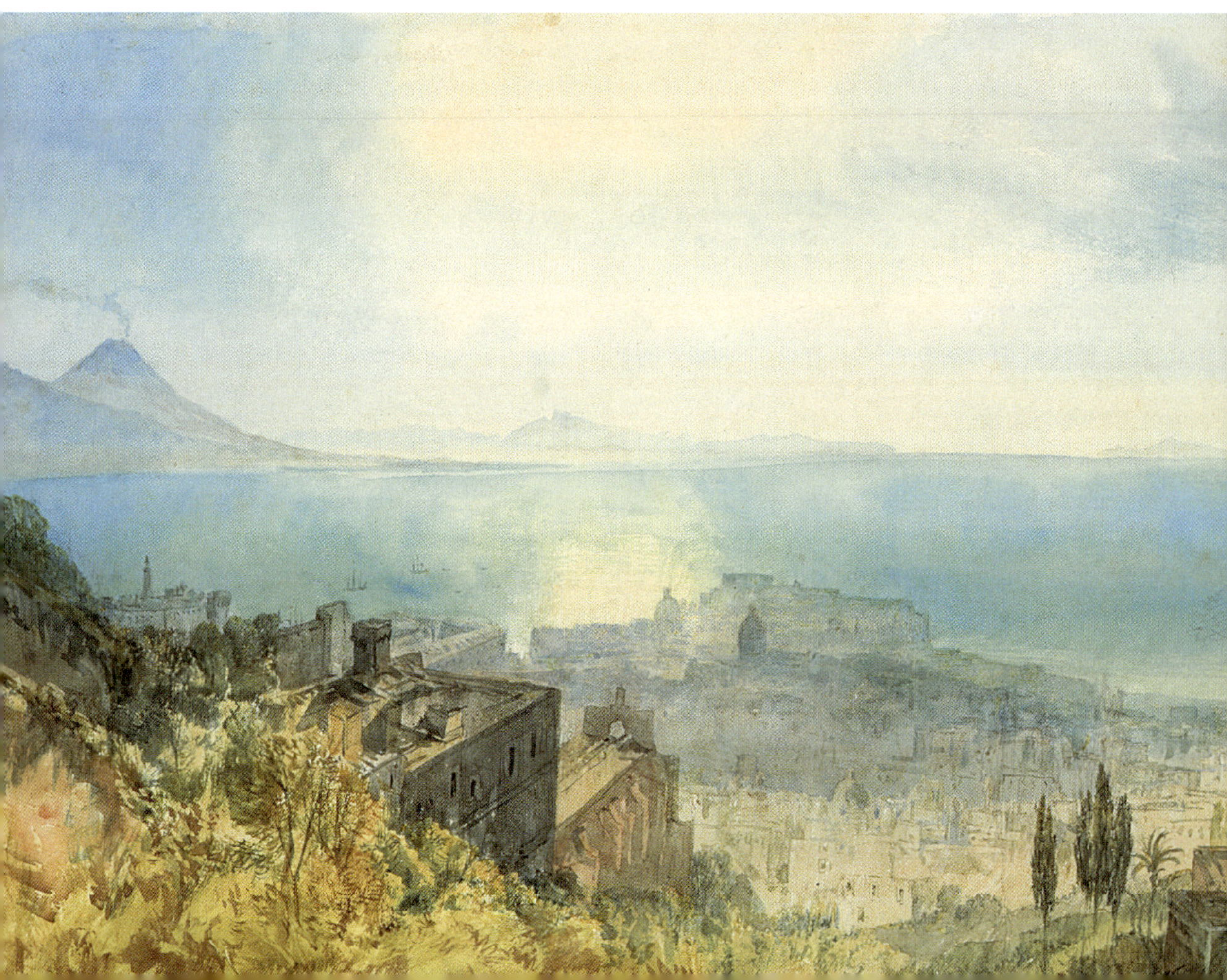

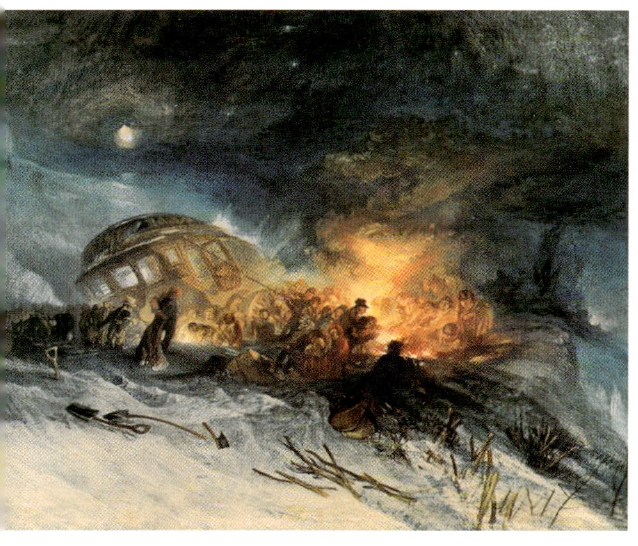

He returned several times to parts of Italy over the next 25 years and held a small exhibition in Rome in 1828. However, these visits were mostly for very short periods as the culmination of tours through Germany or during explorations of Switzerland.

Venice fascinated Turner for years though he spent less than four weeks there during his three visits to the city. He produced many Venetian subjects in later life, evoking its magical setting and mysterious beauty in ethereal oil paintings and delicate watercolours.

Turner's Italian works often contrasted the grandeur of the past with the ruined and neglected appearance of the present. This was a popular theme of the day that he addressed with unique sensitivity and breadth. Both Rome and Venice were once centres of great civilizations. In the age that saw the rise and fall of the self-proclaimed emperor Napoleon, it was inevitable that many saw a parallel with the development, struggles and decline of these famous empires of the past.

— ABOVE —
Messieurs les Voyageurs on their Return from Italy (par la Diligence) in a Snowdrift upon Mount Tarrar – 22nd of January 1829.
This watercolour records a memorable night on Turner's homeward journey from Italy in 1829. The upturned coach and stricken passengers are vividly illuminated by moonlight and firelight.

— RIGHT —
Forum Romanum, for Mr Soane's Museum.
Turner intended this large painting for his architect friend, John Soane, but it was declined on grounds of size. He evokes the heat of Italy through strong colour contrasts and shows a modern Catholic procession among the ruins of the pagan world.

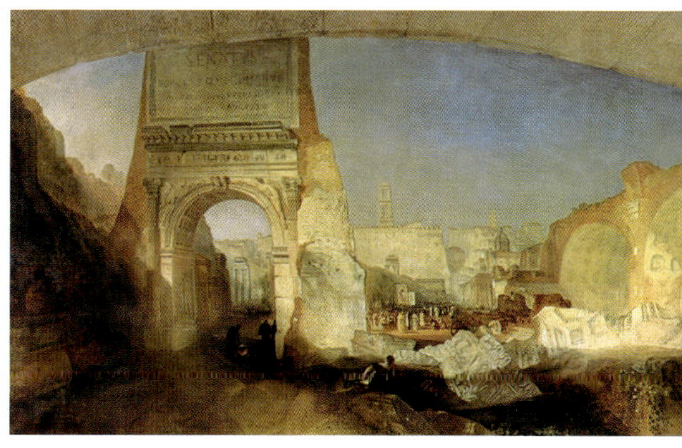

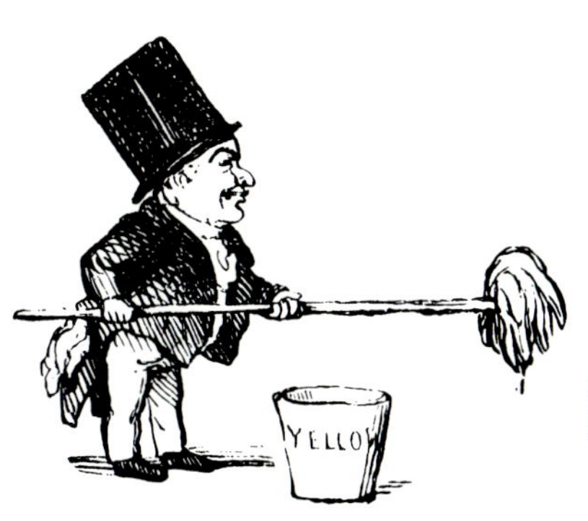

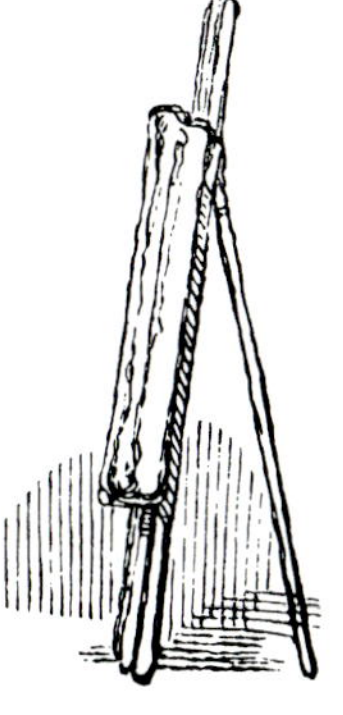

— LEFT —
A cartoon from The Almanack of the Month, *June 1846, suggesting Turner was excessive in his use of the colour yellow.*

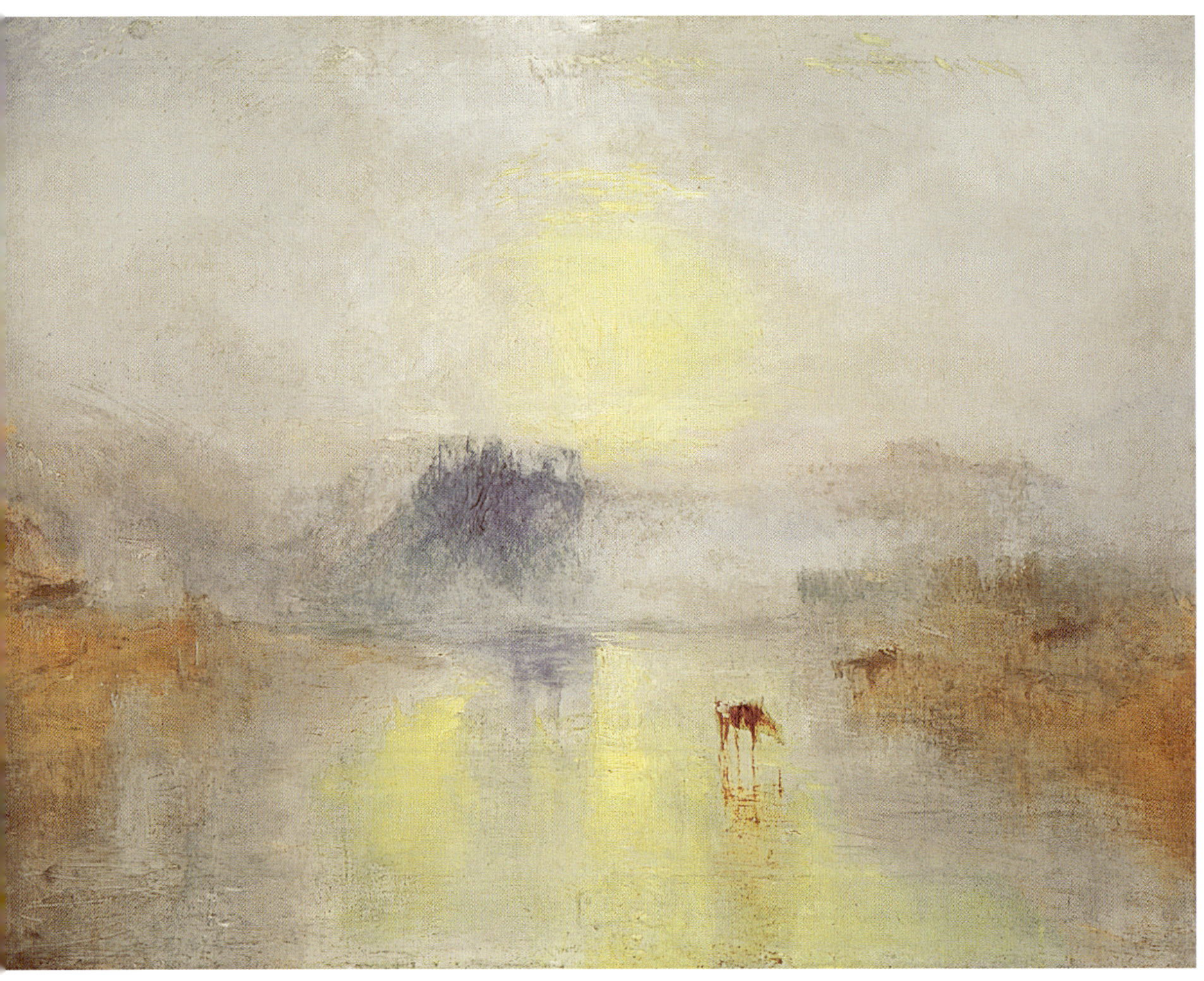

Turner made British tours throughout his life, building a reference library of summer sketches for later work. He drew all kinds of scenery and every effect of British weather. There were few areas he did not reach – by carriage, on horseback, on foot or by boat.

As a landscape artist he was often asked to produce portraits of stately homes, their grounds and environs. In the 1790s, when Turner was still in his early twenties, well-known connoisseurs like William Beckford of Fonthill in Wiltshire and aristocrats like the Lascelles family of Harewood House in Yorkshire were inviting him to make paintings or watercolours of their properties.

Turner was also commissioned to provide scenes for books illustrated with engravings of British views: towns and cities, churches and castles, coasts and rivers, harbours and ports. Having made his tour and drawn hundreds of sketches, he would produce the watercolours back home in London. Sometimes he devised a special journey for the job, but he also used sketches made years, or even decades, earlier.

He had friends and patrons all over Britain and some of his patrons became close friends. Two in particular provided a 'home from home' at opposite ends of England. For many years between 1815 and 1825, Turner was almost a member of the family at Farnley Hall near the grand scenery of Wharfedale in Yorkshire. This was the home of the landowner and politician Walter Fawkes who bought or commissioned over 200 works.

Norham Castle, Sunrise. *Norham Castle on
the River Tweed was a subject Turner painted
many times after first seeing it in 1797. In this
late, unfinished oil only the bare essentials of
the scene are visible: as floating patches of
colour, veiled in morning mist.*

Two Artists in the Old Library, Petworth.
*Turner used the Old Library as his Petworth
studio and painted a series of delightfully
informal sketches of the house. Their charm
and vivacity are largely due to his use
of blue paper and gouache.*

Petworth House in Sussex, a much larger and more splendid building,
is filled with fine works of art and set in a superb park designed by 'Capa-
bility' Brown. The third Earl of Egremont was known as much for his
bohemian lifestyle as for his hospitality, earning Petworth the nickname of
'Liberty Hall'; house parties usually included several artists as well as
hordes of illegitimate children. Turner was a regular and welcome visitor
from about 1827 until the earl's death in 1837.

He never found favour with royalty, however, though he tried hard to
please both George IV and Queen Victoria. Several of his colleagues
received knighthoods and appointments but Turner's art was too visionary
and avant-garde for royal tastes: this must have been a major disappoint-
ment for such an ambitious artist. It was not until 1989 that a work by
Turner, a view of Windsor, entered the Royal Collection.

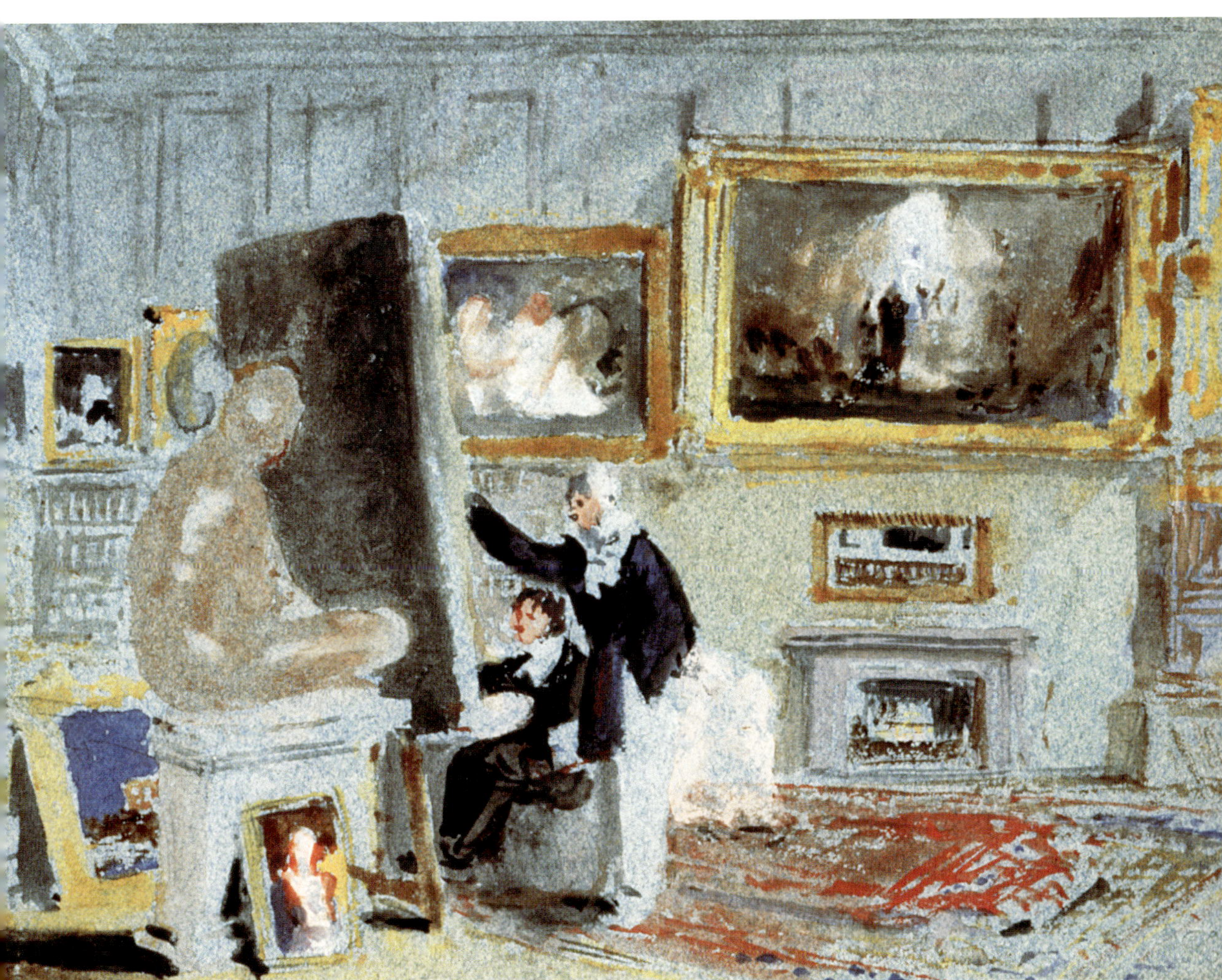

PLEASING THE PUBLIC

The large public exhibitions of the Royal Academy reached only a limited number of people. The same was true of the small one-man shows in the purpose-built gallery at Turner's own house on the corner of Harley Street and Queen Anne Street. Even when the critics acclaimed his paintings, many remained unsold.

However, his art reached a wide public through engravings. These were printed from copper plates or, in the latter part of his career, from the more robust and longer-lasting steel plates. Thanks to new technology, highly complex images could now be printed in thousands rather than hundreds, and an era of peace and prosperity fostered both reading and travel, creating new markets for writers and artists among the growing middle classes.

Turner's colourful scenes were printed in monochrome, using black ink (or occasionally brown). However, his prints have always attracted praise for their technical virtuosity and his ability to suggest colour and mood through sophisticated gradations of light and shade. Turner was a hard taskmaster with his engravers, treating them as translators: he scribbled on proofs and insisted on changes and minute modifications until scenes were exactly right.

Many of his early British views reflected the current vogue for antiquities and medieval buildings as well as for mountains, cliffs and waterfalls. Turner created magnificently dramatic images of the country's most outstanding cathedrals and ruined castles and abbeys.

From around 1810 his British themes often included a patriotic element, with flags waving and soldiers and sailors in the foreground. Turner depicted industry as an integral part of the modern urban scene and a worthy subject in its own right. He celebrated both past and present, enriching innumerable views with well-observed human detail and references to local history and associations.

Some of Turner's engravings were published in the 19th-century equivalent of coffee table books, like the extensive series for *Picturesque Views in England and Wales* in the 1820s and 1830s. Others were issued as individual large prints that could be framed and displayed on the wall.

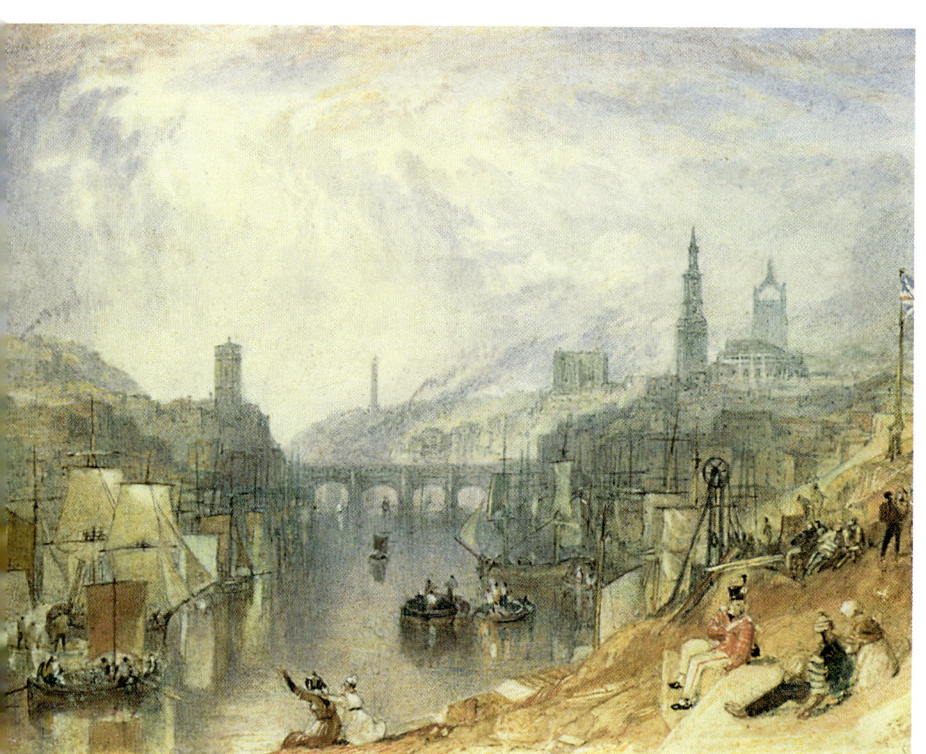

Newcastle-on-Tyne *was engraved in the early 1820s for* The Rivers of England, *a series with subjects ranging from peaceful country views to shipping tossed by the sea. Here Turner shows the modern riverside workers of Gateshead and Newcastle with the historic buildings of their towns in the distance.*

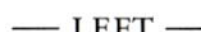

The Bright Stone of Honour (Ehrenbreitstein) and Tomb of Marceau, from Byron's 'Childe Harold'. *Painted specially for engraving in 1835, this scene combines references to war and peace, heroism and poetry. It is dominated by the fortress of Ehrenbreitstein (literally 'broad stone of honour') that guards the confluence of the Rhine and Mosel.*

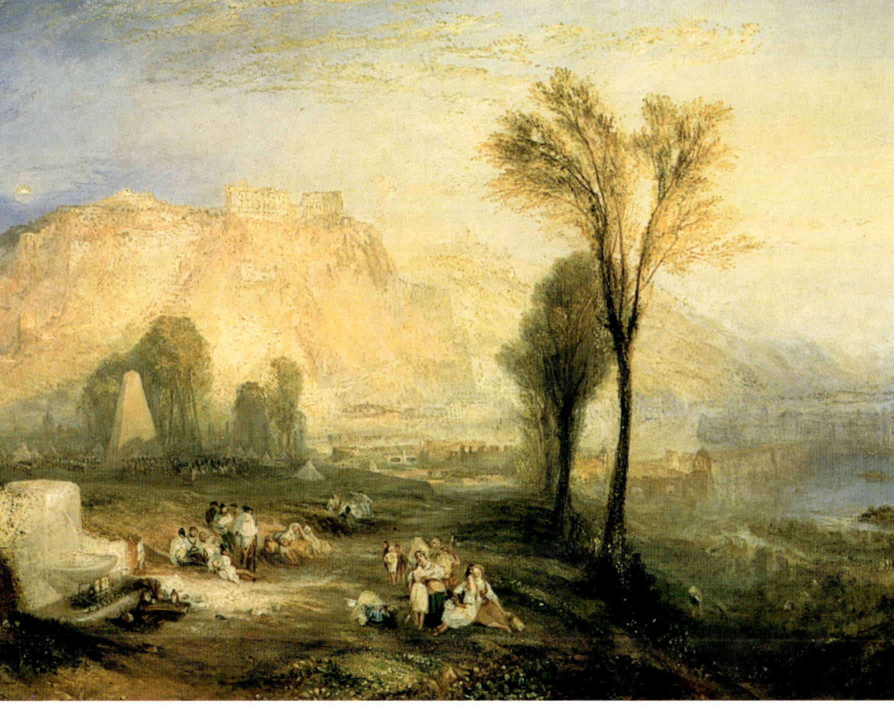

During the 1830s he painted many small watercolours for engraving in literary works, including those illustrating two of the most popular contemporary British writers, Sir Walter Scott (1771–1832) and Lord Byron (1788–1824). He also produced imaginative scenes for reissues of earlier authors including John Milton (1608–74) and John Bunyan (1628–88) and was even called upon to contribute to books on places he had never visited, such as India and the Holy Land.

Turner's engraved work was of such superb quality that it made him famous not only throughout Britain but also in continental Europe and America.

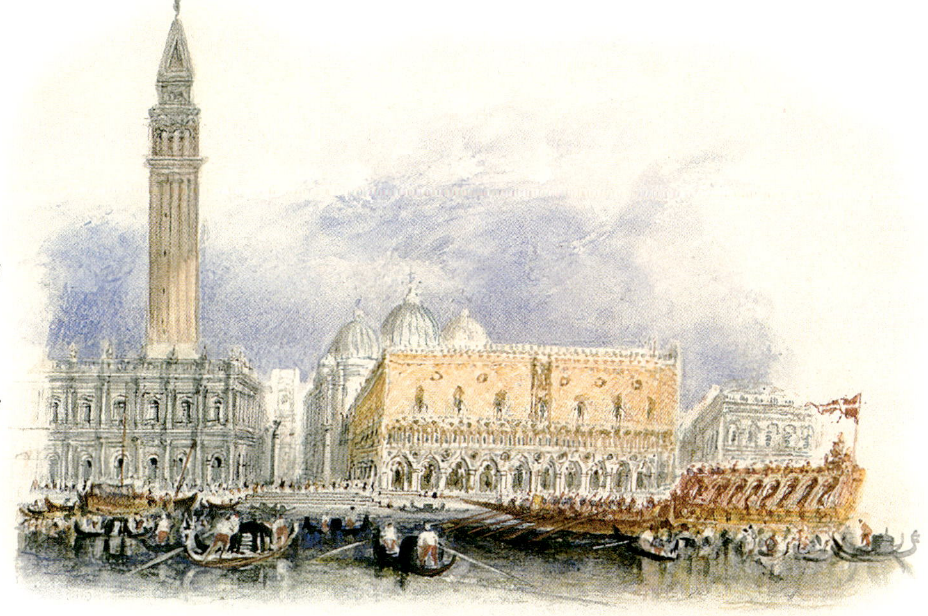

Venice, The Ducal Palace. *Turner's Italian scenes in the work of a minor poet, Samuel Rogers, enchanted thousands of readers, including the 13-year-old John Ruskin. Engraved on a tiny scale, these delicate, borderless vignettes seem to float on the page like evocations of a magic land.*

FRIENDS, FOLLOWERS AND FAMILY

Most of Turner's social life revolved around the Royal Academy, where he exhibited nearly every year and joined in many activities – administrative, charitable and convivial. His colleagues were also good friends, especially the sculptor Francis Chantrey and the painter David Wilkie.

Its exhibition timetable dictated the pattern of Turner's year. The months leading up to April were crucial for preparing fresh exhibits. Once the exhibition had ended in July he was free to leave London, to be 'on the wing' as he put it, staying with friends in the country or travelling abroad.

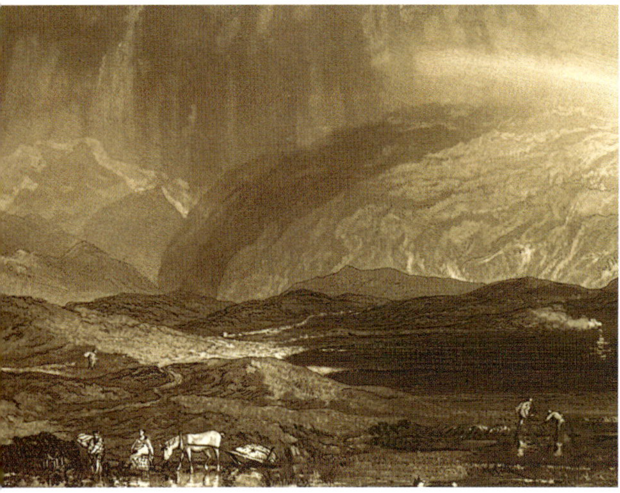

He served as Professor of Perspective at the Academy for over 30 years. While his lectures show his wide knowledge of the subject, his paintings include adventurous departures from the conventions of standard linear perspective. Turner's lectures were infrequent and poorly delivered but were notable for their magnificent diagrams.

He also took his turn in supervising students in the life class and his advice was often sought by aspiring artists.

As a manifesto of his aims, Turner issued a series of illustrations, his *Liber Studiorum* (Book of Studies). There was no text but the prints themselves displayed his mastery of many types of theme, including the sea, history, mountains and architecture. They were issued to subscribers between 1807 and 1819, with Turner himself acting as publisher as well as draughtsman and (to a large extent) engraver. After his lifetime they became widely used in British art education for some 70 years, stimulating discussion and inspiring many artists.

Turner's beloved father provided much practical help in both house and studio, preparing canvases and acting as general factotum. His death in 1829, at the age of 84, came as 'a heavy blow'.

— LEFT —

Peat Bog, Scotland *from Turner's* Liber Studiorum *is a fine example of his extraordinary ability to depict mountain scenery and wild weather. He evokes the Scottish Highlands through stark contrasts of light and shade, combined with vaporous effects suggesting mist and damp.*

— BELOW —

Turner prepared the diagrams for his perspective lectures with enormous care. Interior of the Brocklesby Mausoleum *demonstrates standard perspective applied to curved forms and spaces: an ornate circular room with a coffered and painted dome, classical columns and sculpture, and a geometrically decorated floor.*

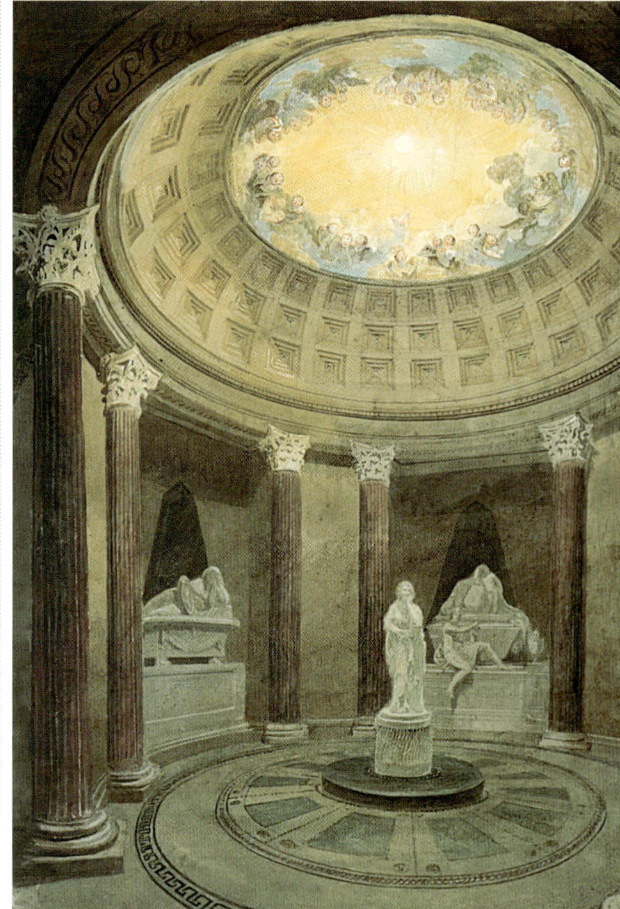

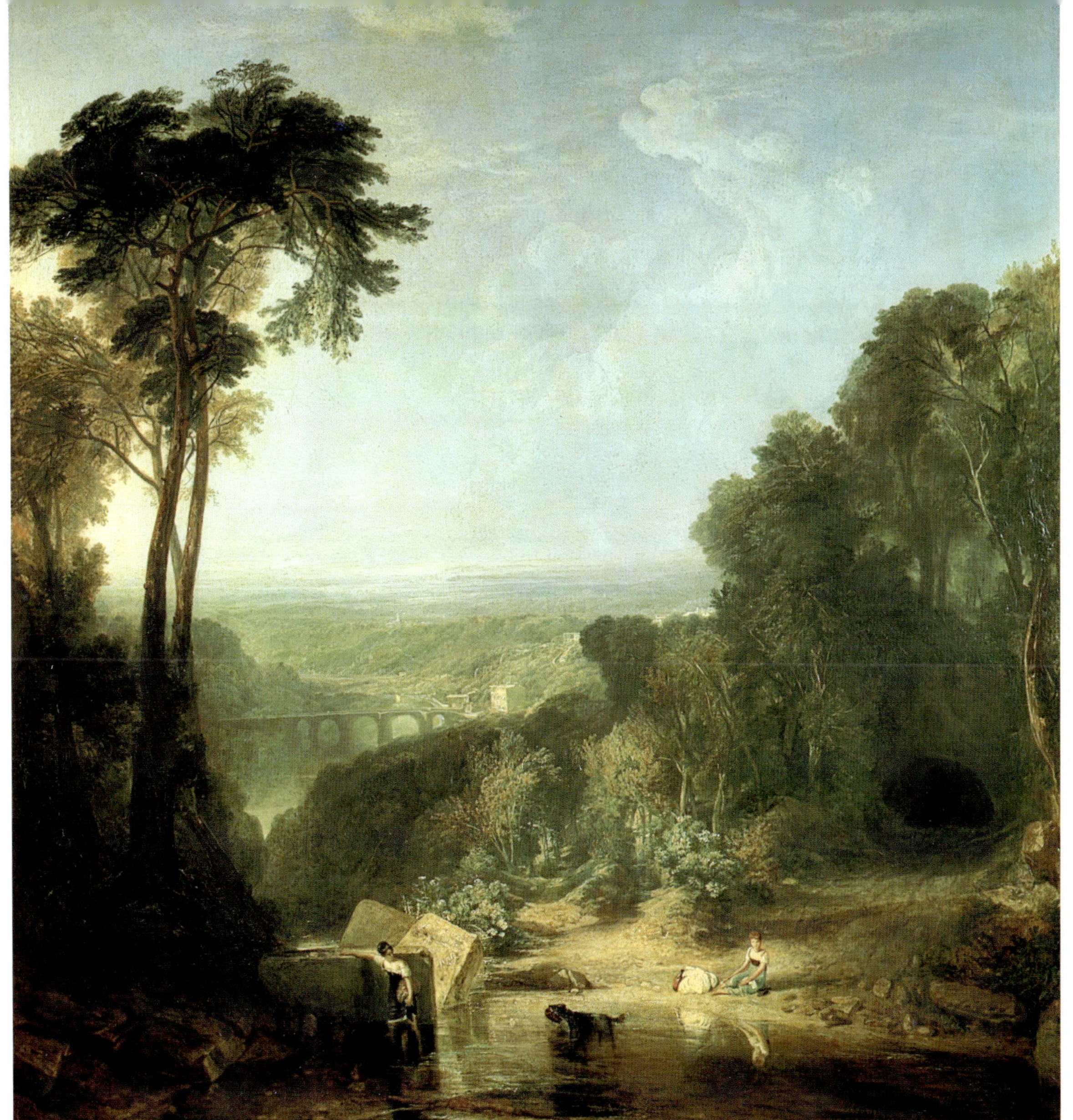

Crossing the Brook. *This imaginary scene, based on sketches of Devon, is composed in the manner of Claude Lorrain, the artist whom Turner most admired. The gradation of colours from foreground to distance shows Turner's superb aerial perspective. The girl in the stream may be his elder daughter, Evelina.*

Work left Turner little time for family life and he never married. However, in 1801 and 1811 he fathered two daughters by Sarah Danby, the widow of the musician John Danby, and the girls were sometimes observed in his house. Later John Danby's unmarried niece, Hannah, served as Turner's housekeeper for over 40 years and admitted visitors to see the paintings in his gallery. In the 1830s Turner met another widow, Sophia Booth, and paid regular visits to her lodging house in Margate for many years. From 1846 onwards she kept house for him in a cottage she had leased overlooking the Thames at Chelsea and she cared for him there in his final illness.

Dort or Dordrecht:
the Dort Packet-Boat from
Rotterdam becalmed.
*This large and luminous
painting of Dordrecht was
inspired not only by Dutch
river scenery but also by the
17th-century Dutch master of
light, Aelbert Cuyp. It is now
in the Yale Center for British
Art, New Haven, USA.*

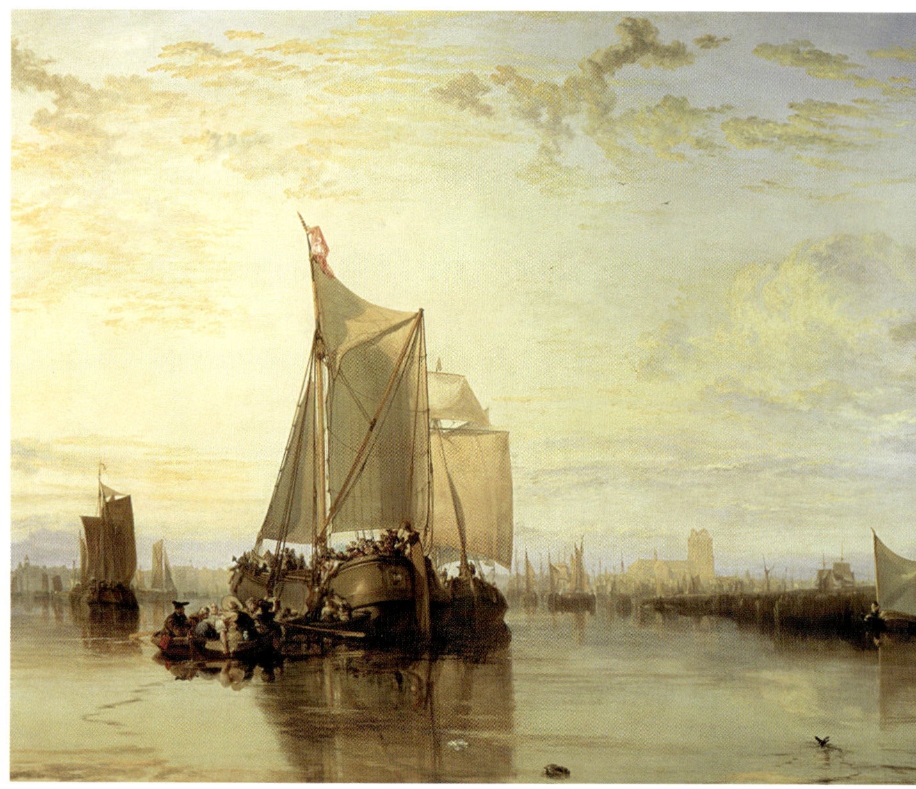

Rivers run through Turner's life and art from the cradle to the grave. His boyhood was spent close to the Thames in central London when roads still led straight to the shore. He died in a riverside cottage in Chelsea where he had a rooftop balcony to enjoy views of water and sky both upstream and downstream.

From about 1805 he rented houses by the Thames west of London, in Isleworth and Hammersmith, as country retreats. He designed his own house in Twickenham, using it intermittently until the 1820s.

Rivers were still important as highways in Turner's day, as they had been for centuries. Roads were often of poor quality, dangerous or non-existent, and progress in horse-drawn vehicles could be extremely slow.

Rivers were also attractive subjects for artists, flowing through towns and villages as well as peaceful stretches of countryside. From Isleworth Turner explored the Thames valley in his own boat, going westward to Oxford and sketching in both watercolour and oil.

Later he often drew quick pencil sketches from the passenger boats in which he travelled, trying to record everything from several viewpoints before it passed.

Turner made journeys along many of the great rivers that flow through Europe, including the Rhine and Danube and their tributaries, and captured the grandeur and variety of their scenery in magnificent oil paintings.

He also made many watercolours of rivers for his patrons and engravers. In 1817 he spent ten days following the most dramatic stretch of the Rhine in Germany, on foot and by boat. Its famous castles and crags, fitful weather and fertile vineyards inspired no less than 50 views, painted that very autumn.

In the 1830s he painted several European rivers in brighter colours and with lighter moods, often using rough blue paper that provided a sparkling basis for both water and sky. Some of these engaging illustrations were reproduced in monochrome in three volumes on the Loire and Seine that were published as New Year giftbooks.

Paris: the Pont Neuf and Ile de la Cité. *Turner's river views often celebrated the dynamism of city life, with water flowing under fine bridges and the hustle and bustle of traffic. His Seine series includes lively depictions of Paris and Rouen.*

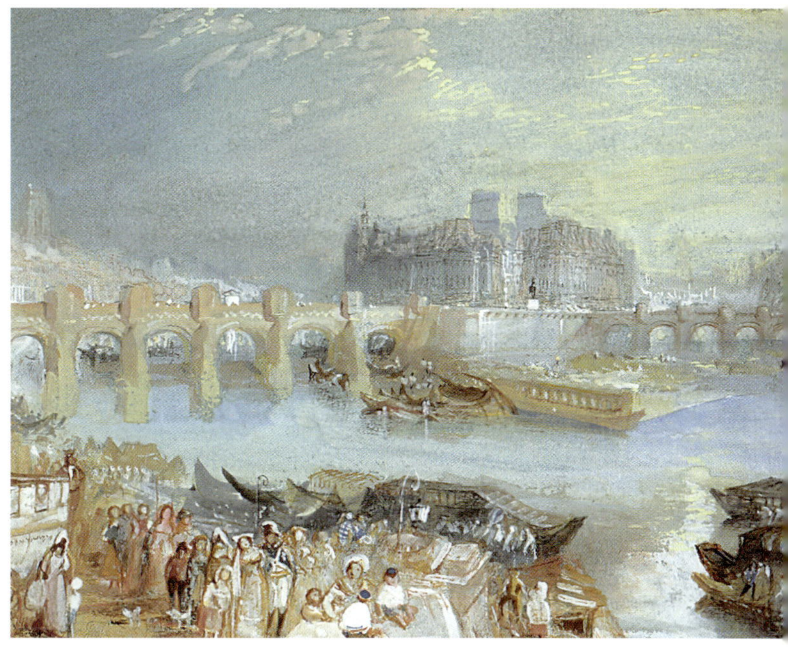

Two of Turner's depictions of the Thames in London are among his most famous works: *The Fighting Temeraire, tugged to her Last Berth to be broken up* (front cover and page 25) and *The Burning of the Houses of Lords and Commons* (page 26). He heightens the drama of these moving and extraordinary occurrences by flooding the surface of the river with reflected light from the setting sun and flaming buildings, showing yet again how a landscape painter should unite every part of the scene into his subject.

Burg Sooneck with Bacharach in the Distance. *The 50 Rhine views of 1817 were painted in watercolour and gouache on paper that Turner had prepared with grey wash to enhance the solemnity of his scenes. They were all bought by Walter Fawkes who also owned* Dort or Dordrecht.

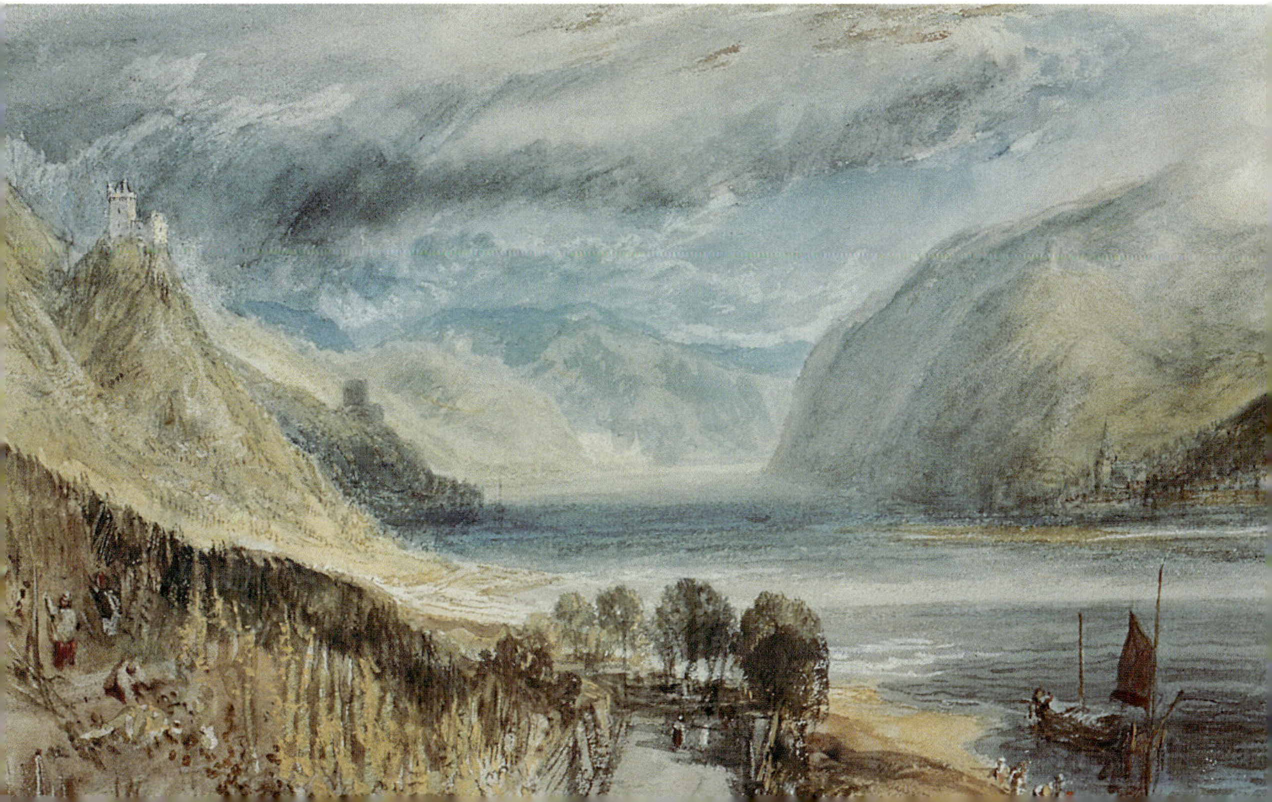

MOUNTAINS AND LAKES

Turner never lost the love of mountains he acquired as a youth exploring Britain – in the Lake District, North Wales and the Highlands of Scotland. The Alps were a lifelong source of inspiration and his late watercolours of Switzerland, painted when he was nearly 70, have always been seen as one of his finest achievements.

He evokes mountains and lakes through washes of colour followed by an apparently infinite number of delicate touches with the smallest of brushes. At one moment forms are hidden behind veils of atmosphere, at another the surface sparkle of the watercolour makes the air itself feel almost tangible.

In Turner's early depictions of mountain areas there was no mistaking the hard physical reality of his subjects, their sheer mass and weight, even when the hills themselves were overlaid with shadows. He was fascinated by geology and well-informed on the subject.

In his late works he seems to be showing insubstantial forms or visionary presences. His last watercolours seem to revel in the ever-shifting effects of sunlight and moonlight on mountains, sky and water.

One of his favourite themes in the 1840s was Lake Lucerne, with its diversity of prospects. He painted it from many viewpoints but his name is especially associated with one view, dominated by the Rigi mountain. Sometimes he shows the Rigi veiled in the shadowy blues of early morning while the pale sun behind it brings golden gleams to the lake. In *The Red Rigi* (above) it is burnished with the red light of sunset as lake and sky return to cool shades of blue and green.

These and many other magical scenes were produced in the most businesslike fashion. After Turner's annual sketching tours of Switzerland, his agent Thomas Griffith circulated a handful of sample scenes to prospective patrons who were given the chance to order a larger version. By now Walter Fawkes, Lord Egremont and other early patrons were dead but Turner enjoyed fresh support from new

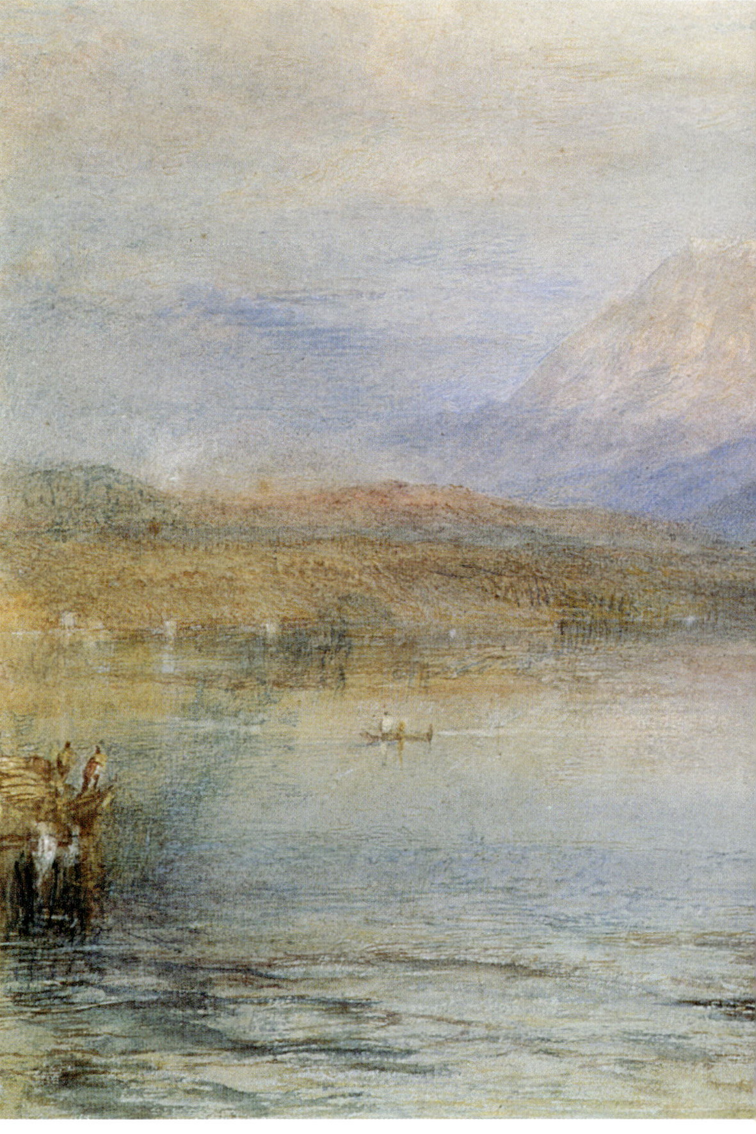

— ABOVE —

One of Turner's most outstanding and atmospheric late watercolours, The Red Rigi *was commissioned by Munro in 1842 and soon afterwards acquired by Ruskin. It is now in the National Gallery of Victoria in Melbourne, Australia.*

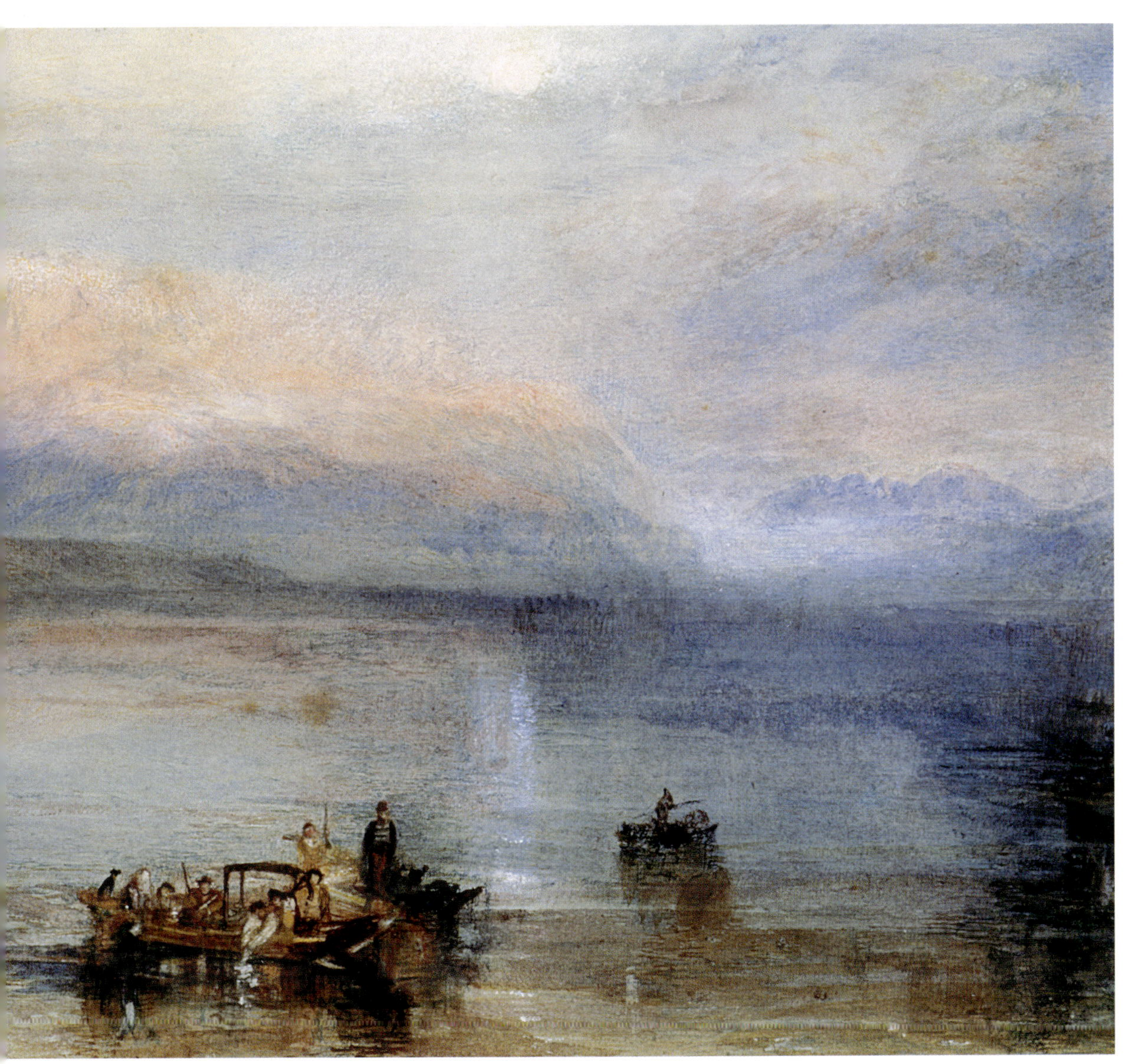

friends and enthusiasts including a Scottish collector, H.A.J. Munro, and the
young John Ruskin (1819–1900).

Turner aimed to complete their orders
before setting off on his next summer journey. In one sense his career had come full
circle: as with his first tour in 1802, his
final tours of Switzerland in the early
1840s were supported by friendship and
the firm assurance of patronage.

— ABOVE —

*In his youth the artist signed himself as
W. or William Turner, but from 1802
he always used J.M.W. Turner.*

THE AGE OF STEAM

Turner lived through an age in which scientific discoveries began to transform Britain as the powers of nature and natural elements were harnessed into use by human ingenuity and invention. The effects of the Industrial Revolution became visible throughout the land, with the arrival of new manufacturing processes and forms of transport. Most were driven by steam, with its attendant outpourings of vapour.

His earliest works show his fascination with light, its sources and effects. These obsessions never left him. At the heart of countless paintings he depicts sun and moon, rainbows, reflections on water, lightning, volcanoes or lamplight. Some contrast the effects of different lights: the red orb of the setting sun and the slender curve of a silvery moon, or the warmth of firelight with the coldness of moonlight. As a young man he depicted the flames of an industrial limekiln against the night sky. Fifty years later he showed a steam train hurtling through rain.

As time went on, his patrons included industrialists with fortunes based on trade and industry. They came not from aristocratic families with country seats but from London itself or the booming cities of Manchester, Birmingham and Liverpool. Their money was earned from such diverse industries as the refining of whale-oil, cotton spinning and the manufacture of steel pens or medical equipment.

Turner himself was fascinated by new inventions. He discussed technicalities with one of the early professional photographers in London and was apparently recorded on daguerreotype in the 1840s, though these images do not survive.

He had scientists, including Michael Faraday, among his acquaintances, and heard about experiments in magnetism and electricity. In one of his most celebrated late pictures (*Snow Storm*, below) the paint is driven around in great swirls and eddies creating a field of energy related to scientific interests of his day.

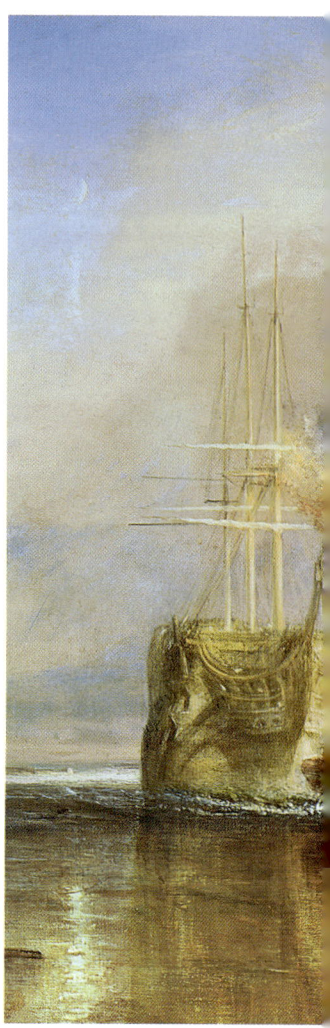

Snow Storm – Steam-boat off a Harbour's Mouth making Signals in Shallow Water, and going by the Lead. The Author was in this Storm on the Night the Ariel left Harwich, *1842. Turner claimed to have been strapped to the mast to study this storm and, even if this was not literally true, he captured its ferocity with unique insight for his time.*

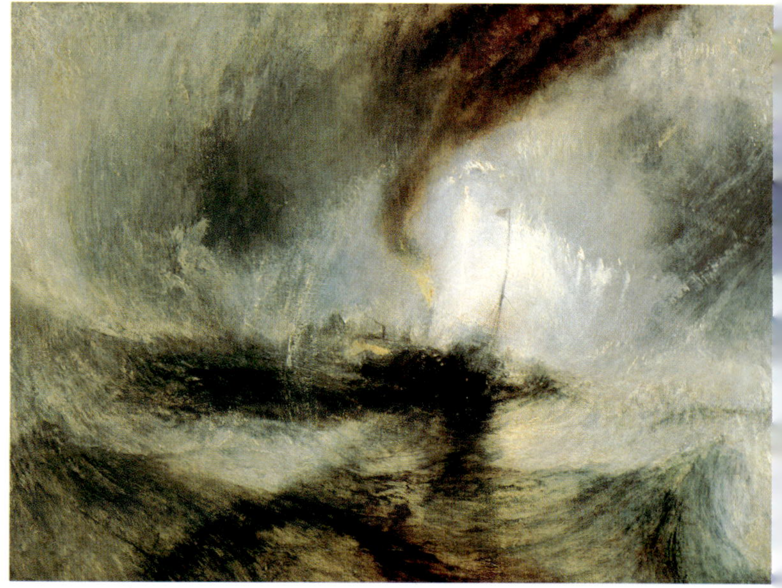

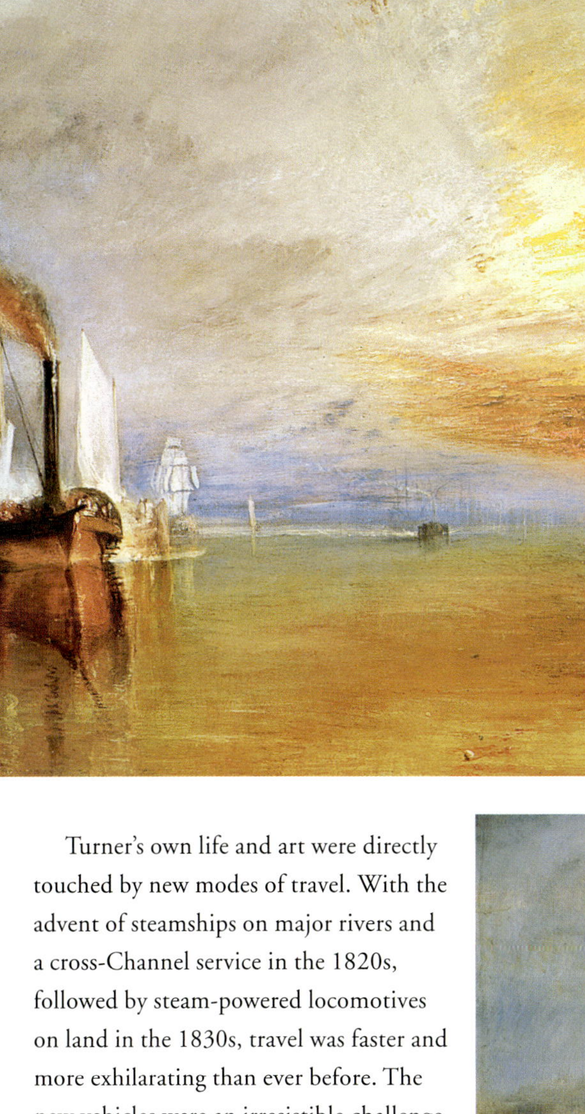

Turner's own life and art were directly touched by new modes of travel. With the advent of steamships on major rivers and a cross-Channel service in the 1820s, followed by steam-powered locomotives on land in the 1830s, travel was faster and more exhilarating than ever before. The new vehicles were an irresistible challenge for a painter, as was the depiction of speed itself. When steamships could defy the power of the ocean and steam trains were revolutionizing travel over land, Turner responded by producing the more intense and powerful mode of artistic expression that the age demanded.

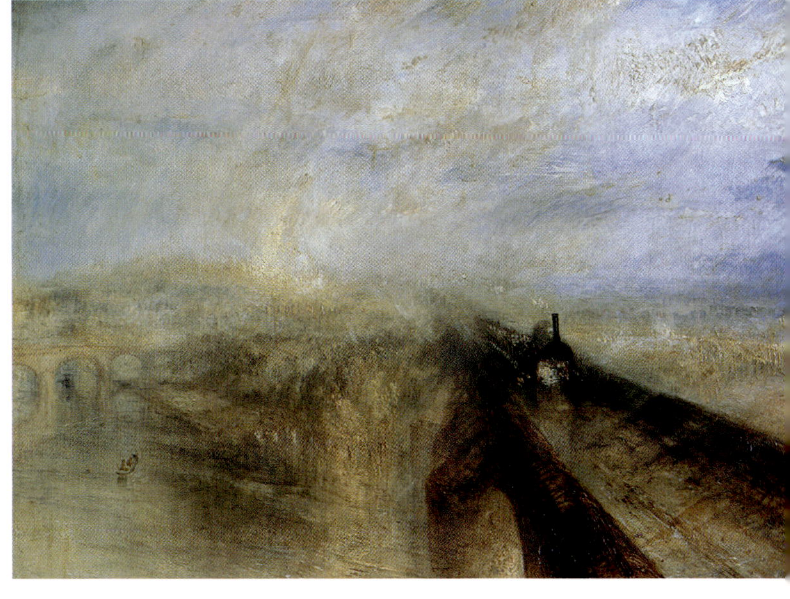

TURNER AND MODERN ART

In his later years Turner became something of a show-man. He enjoyed painting on 'Varnishing Days' when artists were allowed to add finishing touches to their works once they were on the wall of the Academy. Turner went further than this. He would virtually repaint parts of his exhibits, making them much brighter and ensuring they were the most dynamic and conspicuous in the room.

His work has inspired many later artists – not just painters but also writers and musicians. It has been widely discussed, variously interpreted and often misunderstood, but his genius has rarely been challenged.

His art was often too visionary for the critics of his day. Expressions applied to exhibited works included 'pictures of nothing and very like', 'soapsuds and whitewash'. However, his work was ably defended by a young disciple, John Ruskin, who had been overwhelmed by it as a boy. After Turner's death, Ruskin promoted study of his work but its influence has gone further than anything Ruskin imagined: two revolutionary movements in Europe and America are particularly associated with Turner's name.

He is often seen as the father or precursor of Impressionism. Some of his paintings (including *Rain, Steam, and Speed*) were, indeed, known to French Impressionists like Claude Monet and Camille Pissarro in the 1870s. However, they would not have seen his sketches and their ideas and aims were, in fact, very different.

Turner did not share the Impressionists' interest in complementary colours (red and green, blue and orange, yellow and purple), but was concerned with contrasts of warm and cool colours, or dark and light ones. Unlike them, he did not paint large pictures out of doors, quickly and directly from nature. His paintings were produced indoors, slowly and carefully. They were based on detailed sketches and filled with imaginative references.

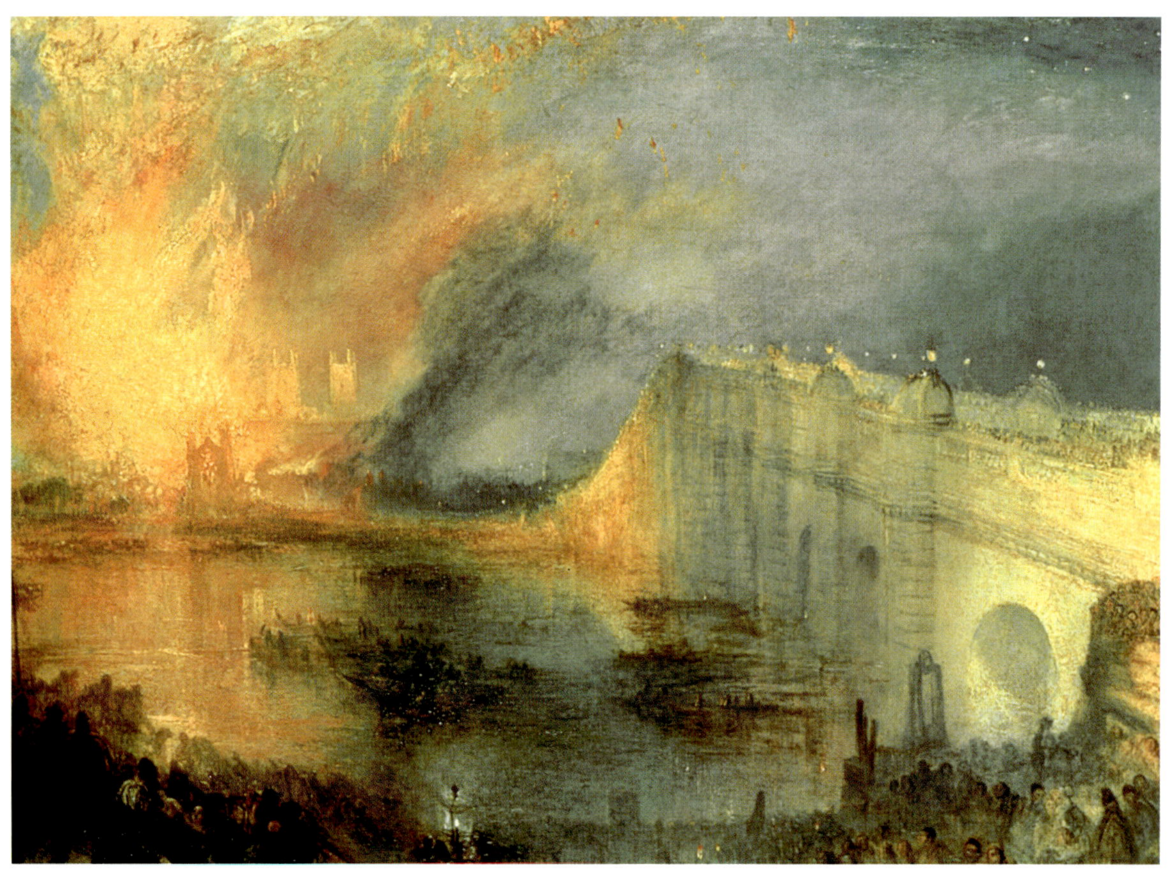

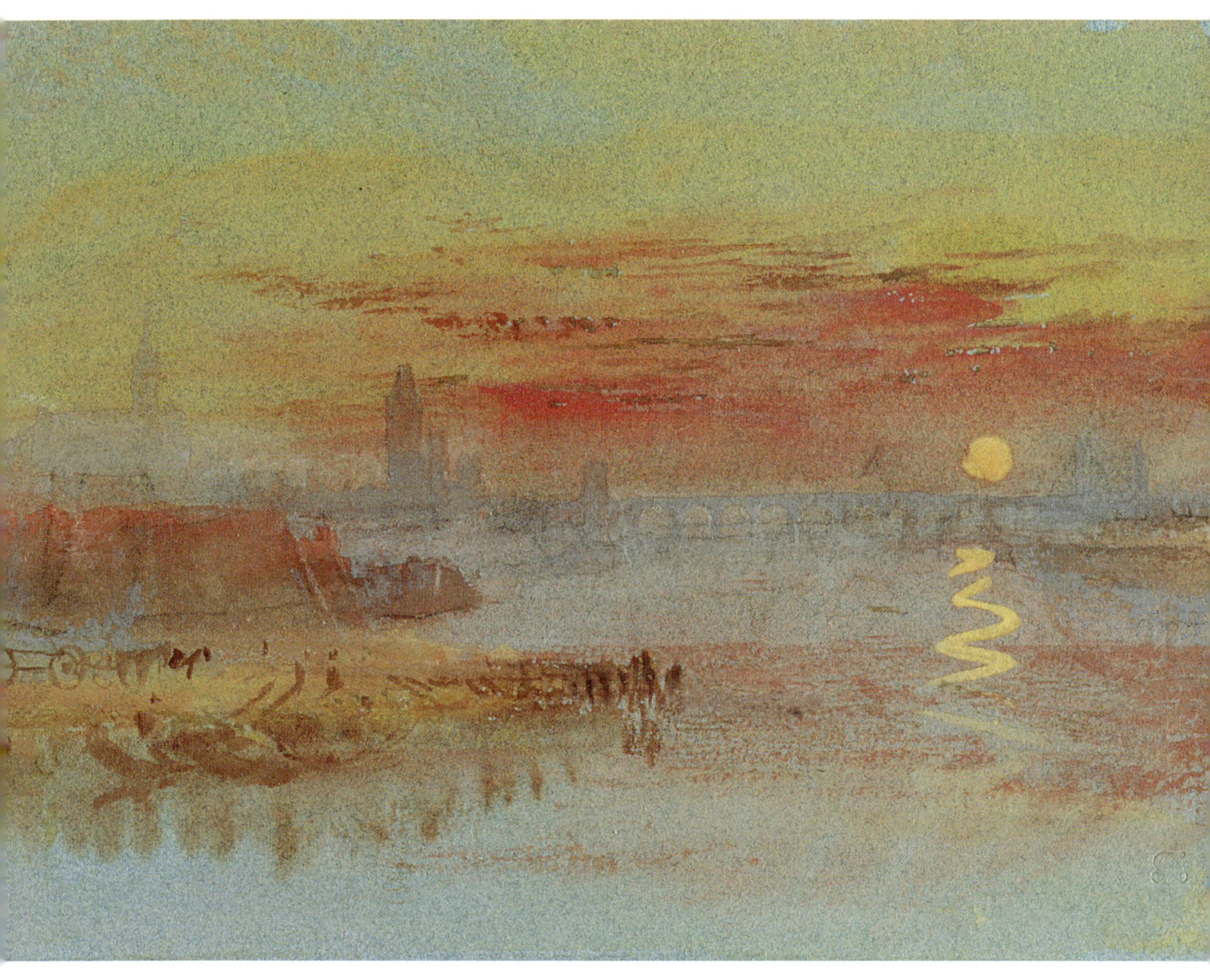

The energetic areas of colour in Turner's late paintings inspired America's Abstract Expressionists in the mid 20th century, especially 'colour field' painters such as Mark Rothko. They saw that Turner had used colour expressively, as a vehicle of human emotion. They recognized the passion in his reds, the grief beyond the black.

Like many artists of today, Turner used his work to comment on contemporary issues. He painted historical scenes with topical relevance as well as modern scenes relating to the Napoleonic wars, political reform, religious tolerance and the abolition of slavery.

Turner's own paintings are famous for their freedom of handling. He discarded conventional colouring and restrictive rules of perspective. Liberty and freedom were not merely fashionable subjects for pictures. They were the very essence of Turner's art.

Turner died in 1851 a very rich man and intended most of his fortune to be used to found a home for destitute artists where his unsold finished oil paintings would be put on public display. This charitable plan was frustrated when his will was challenged by his cousins. The case eventually ended with a compromise in 1856. The family received many of Turner's investments and possessions, the Royal Academy a legacy of £20,000, and the nation (represented by the National Gallery) all his unsold paintings, watercolours and drawings, whether finished or not. Altogether there were nearly 300 oils and around 30,000 works on paper. Today these works are known collectively as the 'Turner Bequest'.

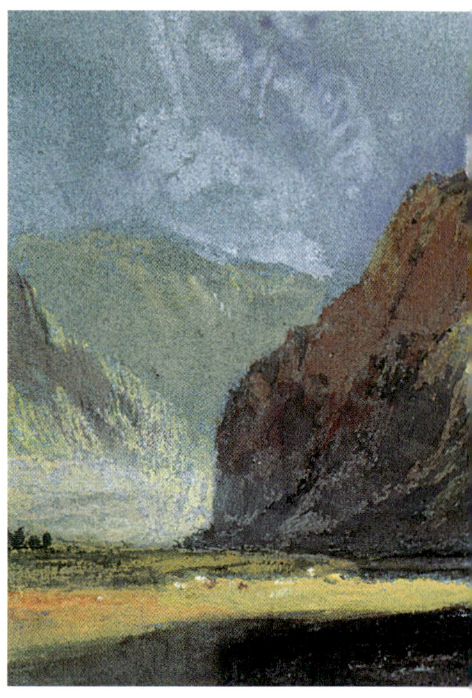

— RIGHT —

The Turner Bequest contains thousands of studies on loose sheets of paper as well as some 300 sketchbooks filled with records and ideas. The Ruined Monastery at Wolf *evokes the placid beauty of the River Mosel through bright contrasts of watercolour and gouache, set off by the blue of the paper.*

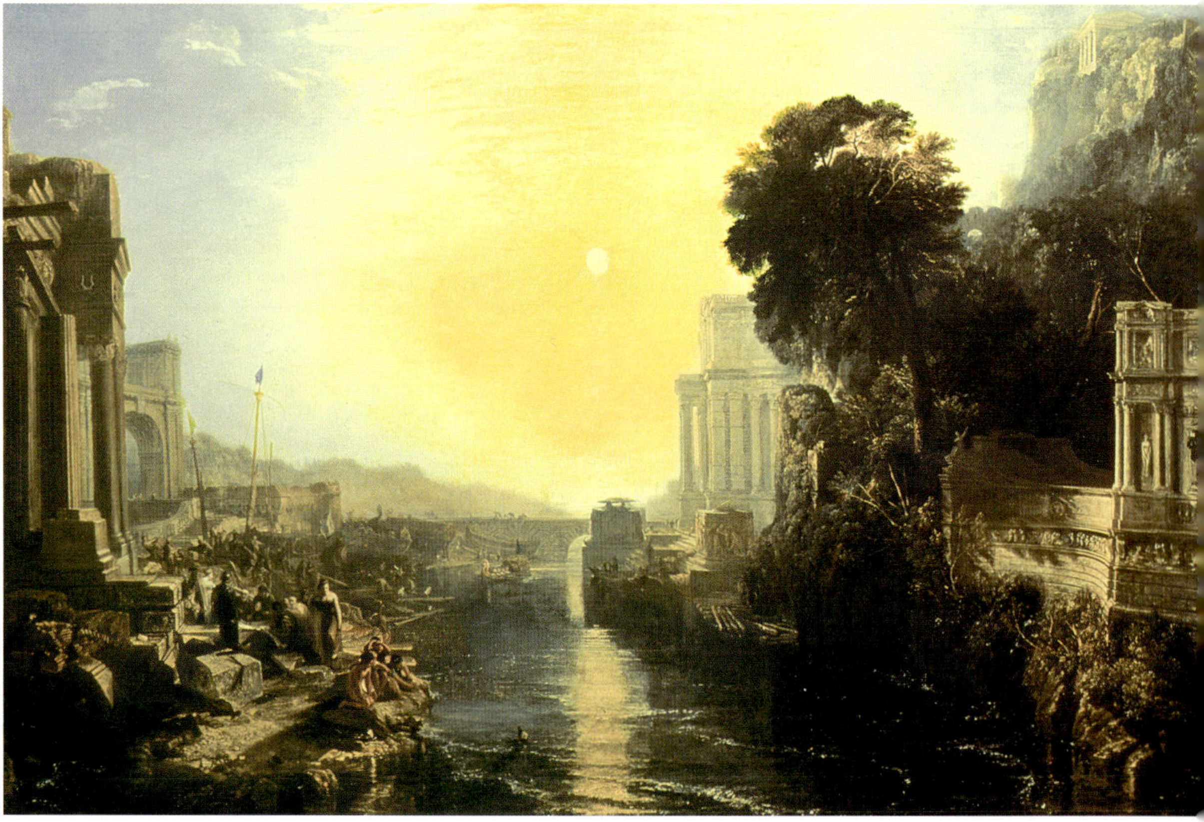